Critical Thinking for Young Children

Unleash the Power of Problem-Solving, Learning Strategies and Key Educational Skills as a Guide to Raising Smart Kids Who Teach Themselves

Nicholas Bright

© **Copyright 2024 - All rights reserved.**

The content of this book may not be reproduced, copied, or transmitted without explicit written permission from the author(s) or publisher. Doing so would constitute a breach of copyright law and could result in serious legal repercussions for any party participating in the illicit reproduction of the material. Furthermore, due to the nature of intellectual rights, it is impossible to duplicate or replace the original work produced by the author(s) or publisher; therefore, the only way to legally gain access to this content is through direct authorization from either party.

The publisher and the author(s) of this book shall not be held accountable in any way for any damages, reparations, ill health, or financial losses that may arise because of the information contained herein, either directly or indirectly. This includes any potential harm, monetary loss, or other consequences from individuals' usage of said information. It is also understood that these individuals will not be able to use this clause to evade legal responsibility for their wrongdoings related to the content provided in this book. The publisher and author(s) will thus be free from all liabilities associated with the publication and distribution of this book.

All trademarks, whether registered or pending, are the property of their respective owners.

Legal Notice

This book is subject to copyright protection and should only be used for personal use. Furthermore, it should not be shared with any other individual or persons for any purpose other than that for which it was initially intended. It is strictly prohibited to amend, reproduce, distribute, utilize, quote, or paraphrase any part of the content within this publication without prior authorization from the writer or publisher. Any violation of these regulations may result in legal action against those who have breached them.

Disclaimer Notice

The presented work is strictly informational and should not be interpreted as an offer to buy or sell any form of security, instrument, or investment vehicle. Furthermore, the information contained herein should not be taken as a medical, legal, tax, accounting, or investment recommendation given by the author(s) or any affiliated company, employees, or paid contributors. In other words, the information is presented without considering individual preferences for specific investments in terms of risk parameters. It is general information that does not account for a person's lifestyle and financial objectives. It is important to note that no tailored advice will be provided based on the given information.

Table of Contents

PREFACE 15

Nurturing Critical Thinking in Early Childhood: A Guide for Parents, Educators, and Caregivers 15

INTRODUCTION 18

CHAPTER 1: THE AWAKENING MIND: UNLEASHING EARLY CRITICAL POWER 21

Why Early Critical Thinking Skills are Your Child's Best Tool for Tomorrow 21
    Unleashing Early Critical Power 25

CHAPTER 2: FROM THEORY TO PLAY: BRIDGING THE GAP IN EARLY EDUCATION 31

Unleashing the Power of Play: Transform Early Learning Today 31

Step-by-Step Guide: "Playful Minds Framework" 34
    Step 1: Understanding Cognitive Development Theories 34
    Step 2: Translating Theory into Playful Activities 34
    Step 3: Hands-On Experiences for Abstract Concepts 35
    Step 4: Incorporating Playful Learning Strategies 35
    Step 5: Reflecting on Theory-to-Play Connections 35

Embracing Hands-On Learning: Practical Resources for Early Childhood Education 37

The Playful Learning Framework 39
    Core Principles Application 39

Social Learning Integration 40
Material Selection and Adaptation 40
Evaluation Strategies 41

CHAPTER 3: THINKING CRITICALLY ABOUT TOMORROW: CONNECTING SKILLS WITH REAL LIFE 43

From Theories to Tangible Tasks: How Can We Make Critical Thinking Accessible to Children? 43

Enhancing Problem-Solving with Real-Life Examples and Case Studies 47

Bridging Theory to Practice 51
Taking Action 52

CHAPTER 4: DIGITALLY WIRED TO THINK: LEVERAGING TECHNOLOGY FOR CRITICAL MINDS 53

Harnessing Digital Tools to Cultivate Young Critical Thinkers 53

Leveraging Interactive Technology for Critical Thinking in Early Education 57

CHAPTER 5: LEARNING UNLEASHED: EMBRACING DIVERSITY IN CRITICAL EDUCATION 63

Harness the Power of Technology in Early Childhood Education ... 63

Cultivating Critical Thinkers through Inclusive Teaching Strategies 66

CHAPTER 6: EVERY DAY, EVERY WAY: INTEGRATING CRITICAL THOUGHT INTO LIFE 72

Transforming Everyday Moments into Opportunities for Growth ... 72

Fostering Creativity, Flexibility, and Resilience in Critical Thinking Skills 75

    Practical Strategies 79
    Continuous Challenges 79
    Culture of Inquiry 80

CHAPTER 7: TRACKING THE THINKER: MEASURING CRITICAL PROGRESS 81

Unveiling the Blueprint: A Strategic Approach to Cultivating Young Critical Thinkers 81

Setting Milestones: Navigating the Journey of Cognitive Growth 83

Crafting Critical Thinkers: A Step-by-Step Guide 83

    Step 1: Grasping Significance 83
    Step 2: Methods in Action 84
    Step 3: Keeping Track 84
    Step 4: Milestone Mapping 84
    Step 5: Celebrate Growth 84

Evaluating Critical Thinking Progress in Early Childhood Education 86

Evaluation Framework: Critical Thinking Development Model 88

    Definition of Critical Thinking Milestones 89
    Observing Behaviors and Skills 89
    Informal Assessments 89
    Quantitative Measures 90
    Self-Assessment and Reflection 90

Constructive Feedback 90
Setting Realistic Goals 91
Assess, Adapt, Achieve 91
Celebrate Every Step 92
Foster Creativity and Resilience 92
Take Action 92

CHAPTER 8: BEYOND THE BOX: CULTIVATING CREATIVE PROBLEM-SOLVERS 94

Unleashing Creative Minds: A Blueprint for the Future 94

Nurturing Flexible Thinking in Young Minds 98

Cultivating Creative Problem-Solvers: A Necessity, Not an Option 101
Tracking Progress is Key 101
Implement Practical Solutions 102
Empower Through Action 102
Engage with Confidence 102

CHAPTER 9: ENGAGING YOUNG MINDS: THE KEY TO PRACTICE AND RETENTION 104

Unleashing the Power of Play: Transforming Theory into Thrilling Learning Adventures 104

Crafting Customized Cognitive Challenges 106

A Blueprint for Building Better Thinkers 107
Step by Step: "Cognitive Constructors" 107

Enhancing Learning Retention through Practical Activities 111

CHAPTER 10: READING FOR REASONING: BUILDING A FOUNDATION WITH BOOKS 116

Unlocking the Mind: How Books Shape Our Youngest Thinkers .. 116

Reading as a Tool for Cognitive Development 119
   Nurturing Analytical Thinking.. 119
   Building a Foundation for Reasoning... 120
   Embracing the Journey Towards Critical Thinking 120

CHAPTER 11: LEARNING REIMAGINED: INNOVATIVE APPROACHES TO THINKING........ 126

Are You Ready to Transform How Your Child Thinks? 126

Recognize the Importance of Novelty in Maintaining Children's Engagement in Learning Activities 130
   Embracing Novelty as a Catalyst for Engagement.................................. 131
   The Power of Surprise and Innovation.. 131
   Balancing Familiarity With Novelty.. 132
   Practical Strategies for Integrating Novelty.. 132

Framework: Innovative Teaching Model for Critical Thinking Development 133
   Identifying Interests and Curiosities... 133
   Thematic Learning Integration.. 134
   Creating Immersive Learning Environments... 134
   Incorporating Technology and Balancing Screen Time 135
   Encouraging Reflection and Discussion 135
   Practical Implications.. 135

CHAPTER 12: THE GAME CHANGER: STIMULATING MINDS WITH PLAY 138

Igniting Young Minds: The Transformative Power of Play in Learning 138

Nurturing Critical Thinking Through Cognitive Games 142

The Importance of Innovative Teaching Methods 145
   Actionable Strategies for Enhanced Cognitive Development.............. 146
   Encouragement to Take Initiative 146
   Foster Curiosity and Exploration 147

CHAPTER 13: CRAFTING INQUISITIVE THINKERS: THE ROLE OF THE GUIDING ADULT 148

Unlocking the Potential of Young Minds Through Strategic Play .. 148

Cultivating Critical Thinking in a Supportive Learning Environment 152

CHAPTER 14: TOMORROW'S THINKERS: NURTURING RESILIENT AND ADAPTABLE MINDS 158

Empowering Tomorrow's Leaders: The Indispensable Role of Early Critical Thinking 158

Nurturing Critical Thinking for Future Success 162

EPILOGUE 169

The Journey Forward: Empowering Young Minds 169

CONCLUSION 172

BONUS MATERIAL 175

Your Questions, Answered! 175
   1.   How Do You Differentiate Between Teaching Critical Thinking Skills and Traditional Teaching Methods? 175

2. Can Critical Thinking Skills Be Taught to Children of Any Age, or Is There an Ideal Age to Start? 177
3. What Are the Most Common Barriers Parents and Educators Face When Trying to Instill Critical Thinking in Children? 178
4. How Can Technology Be Used Effectively to Enhance Critical Thinking Skills in Early Childhood? 180
5. Are There Specific Activities or Games That Can Help Develop Critical Thinking Skills in Young Children? 182
6. What Role Does Emotional Intelligence Play in Developing Critical Thinking Abilities? 184
7. How Can We Measure the Development of a Child's Critical Thinking Skills Over Time? 186
8. In What Ways Can Caregivers Integrate Critical Thinking Exercises Into Everyday Routines? 188
9. What Are Some Examples of Critical Thinking Milestones We Should Expect at Different Developmental Stages? 189
10. How Can Critical Thinking Skills Help Children With Learning Difficulties or Special Education Needs? 191
11. Can You Provide Strategies for Teaching Critical Thinking to Highly Gifted Children? 193
12. How Does the Approach to Teaching Critical Thinking Differ Across Cultural Contexts? 195
13. What Impact Does a Multi-Lingual Environment Have on the Development of Critical Thinking Skills in Children? 197
14. Are There Any Recommended Resources or Tools for Parents and Educators to Continue Their Own Education in Teaching Critical Thinking? 199
15. How Can Schools and Communities Collaborate to Create an Environment That Fosters Children's Critical Thinking From an Early Age? 201

Welcome to the

Ideas Worth Sharing

Series

My name is Nicholas Bright, and I've spent nearly two decades working as a psychologist specializing in Behavioral Neuroscience and Interpersonal Communication in the US, UK, and Australia. Throughout my career, I've encountered countless stories, experiences, and insights that have shaped my understanding of the human mind and interpersonal interactions.

This series is a collaborative effort, bringing together the experience and expertise of myself and my colleagues: Erica May, Jeff Sharpe, Camila Alvarez, and potentially new faces in the future! We've chosen to write under pen names to respect everyone's privacy and keep the spotlight on the valuable content we offer rather than us as individuals. This decision allows us to freely share our knowledge without the distractions that often come with the limelight. We stand by the authenticity and credibility of the content shared here—our professional integrity remains at the forefront of this series.

We are deeply passionate about our field, and our primary goal is to equip you with practical, research-backed insights that you can implement in your everyday life. Each chapter is designed to inspire and help you better understand yourself and those around you.

We invite you to engage actively with the material: take notes, discuss the ideas with friends and family, and, most importantly, apply the lessons in your daily routine.

1. **Read;** understand what can be done to improve
2. **Reflect;** appreciate your feelings and their origins
3. **Remember;** put your learning into action

Thank you for embarking on this journey of knowledge and growth with us,

Nick

Want to Win Free Books?

Join Our Newsletter!

In this series, we appreciate that someone may find many different books helpful. I certainly know that when discussing sensitive topics like, for example, divorce, we can end up working on grief, anxiety, self-confidence, cognitive dissonance, and lots more. When we encounter a major challenge in life, it is rarely due to one small problem but rather a concoction of our experiences, outlooks, and actions; it's often a deep-rooted issue with many different things we need to uncover and support. We are complicated beings, and we must recognize this. As such, I would love to invite you all to join our newsletter.

In this, I aim to write articles of interest, including excerpts from various books in the series, as well as **vouchers**, **discounts**, and **giveaways**—and of course, no gimmicks or catches. I harbor a deep loathing of companies that offer seemingly amazing deals, only to charge you vast amounts in hidden fees! I vowed to never fall into that trap myself, and any offers I make are designed to be of true benefit and help. If you win a book in a giveaway, I want you to read it with a smile.

Join our newsletter and discover the additional value we can add to your life's curriculum!

Join us at: **www.IdeasWorthSharingSeries.com/newsletter**

See you on the inside!

About the Author: Dr. Nicholas Bright

Dr Nicholas Bright, a highly esteemed Clinical Psychologist based in the vibrant city of New York, is devoted to preventing and treating mental health problems. Nicholas earned his Clinical Psychology degree from Syracuse University, nestled in the heart of New York State. His practice is centred around mindfulness-based therapies, humanistic approaches, and positive psychology principles, enabling individuals to discover their potential and build emotional and psychological resilience.

He has maintained professional ties and a personal friendship with Erica May since their university years. Together, in the Ideas Worth Sharing series, they aim to extend their therapeutic expertise beyond their clinical settings through a series of books on critical psychological topics. This series will delve into various mental health themes, offering comprehensive advice on integrating emotional balance and humanistic practices into everyday life and techniques for fostering positive mental health.

By sharing practical examples and insights from his clinical work, Nick intends to make evidence-based psychological concepts accessible to the general public. His ultimate goal is to empower individuals with the knowledge and tools to manage their mental health effectively, enhance overall well-being, and build resilience.

Preface

"The greatest discoveries of science have always been those that forced us to rethink our beliefs about the universe and our place in it."

Robert L. Park

Nurturing Critical Thinking in Early Childhood: A Guide for Parents, Educators, and Caregivers

In the delicate tapestry of early childhood, every thread of experience and learning shapes the vibrant patterns that will define an individual's entire life. This book is dedicated to critical thinking, one of the most crucial aspects of that developmental stage. Here, we delve into the transformative power of nurturing critical thinking from a tender age, providing parents, educators, and caregivers with the tools they need to mold young minds prepared for a world brimming with wonders.

The decision to pen these pages stemmed from a simple yet profound realization: while numerous resources focus on general cognitive development, few tackle the nuanced art of fostering critical thinking in preschool-aged children. Observing this gap, I felt compelled to create a guide that demystifies this process, making it accessible and actionable. Through this book, I aim to bridge the theoretical frameworks of cognitive development with practical, everyday activities that are engaging and effective.

Imagine a parent watching their child navigate a complex puzzle or an educator guiding little learners through a thought-provoking story. These are moments and opportunities to ignite a lifelong passion for inquiry and problem-solving. Such scenarios inspired me to collect these insights and strategies, hoping they serve as beacons for those who guide our youngest thinkers.

This journey has been shaped significantly by the wisdom of pioneers in educational psychology and the heartfelt stories shared by fellow educators and parents. Their experiences and challenges added depth and urgency to this endeavor, underscoring the need for an insightful and practical resource.

I am profoundly grateful to you, the reader, for choosing to embark on this journey through these pages. Your commitment to enhancing the lives of children through education is both noble and essential. This book is crafted for you—a parent, educator, or caregiver—who seeks to teach and inspire.

You will find that no prior expertise in educational theory is needed to apply the ideas discussed here. All that is required is a desire to make a difference in the lives of young children by fostering an environment rich in challenges and opportunities for critical exploration.

Thank you for your trust in this work. As you turn each page, may you find valuable insights and practical strategies that resonate with your experiences and aspirations. Let's continue together on this path towards nurturing minds capable of thinking critically about their world—minds that will one day shape our future.

Introduction

"The essence of the independent mind lies not in what it thinks, but in how it thinks."

Christopher Hitchens

In a world that's evolving at an unprecedented pace, nurturing young minds has never been more critical. This book is a compass for those at the helm of this challenging yet rewarding endeavor. It is a guiding light for parents, educators, and caregivers committed to fostering an environment that encourages academic success and cultivating the foundational skills necessary for lifelong learning and personal fulfillment.

The significance of critical thinking in early childhood cannot be overstated. It goes beyond the mere accumulation of knowledge, tapping into the essence of understanding, problem-solving, and creativity. This book underscores the importance of laying a solid foundation for critical thinking from a young age, highlighting how such skills prepare children for academic achievements and the complexities of the real world.

Through its pages, you'll find a rich tapestry of strategies, activities, and insights aimed at integrating critical thinking into the daily interactions with preschool-aged children. These approaches are meticulously designed to kindle curiosity, enhance cognitive development, and boost confidence without overwhelming or underestimating the capabilities of young learners.

The journey towards fostering critical thinking is depicted as profound and enlightening for the children and those who guide them. It is presented as an opportunity to witness and contribute to the extraordinary process of growth and discovery that unfolds uniquely in each child. This narrative is a hearty invitation to fully immerse oneself in early childhood education's intricacies and wonders.

The book also addresses the inevitable evolution of the job market and the increasing importance of adaptability, problem-solving, and analytical thinking skills. It argues convincingly for the early introduction of critical thinking skills to future-proof our children's careers, ensuring they emerge as innovative, dynamic, and resilient societal contributors.

Beyond developing cognitive skills, the text strongly emphasizes cultivating a mindset of continuous improvement and a love for learning. This mindset, it argues, transcends academic boundaries and infuses every aspect of life, preparing children to thrive in an unpredictable world.

The practical strategies detailed within are not presented as an exhaustive list but as a starting point. The book encourages ongoing exploration, experimentation, and adaptation of novel ideas in keeping with the evolving field of early childhood education.

As a call to action, this introduction aims to galvanize parents, educators, and caregivers into taking decisive steps toward integrating critical thinking into their daily routines with children. It highlights the transformative power of small, consistent actions in shaping young learners' intellectual and emotional development.

Concluding with the poetic wisdom of William Butler Yeats, the introduction sets the tone for a book that seeks not just to educate but to inspire. It is an invitation to light the spark of curiosity and critical thinking in young minds, illuminating a path toward a future replete with endless possibilities and hope. This book is a testament to the belief that education is not merely about filling minds with information but about igniting the fires of inquiry, creativity, and passion for learning.

Chapter 1: The Awakening Mind: Unleashing Early Critical Power

"Education is not the learning of facts, but the training of the mind to think."

Albert Einstein

Why Early Critical Thinking Skills are Your Child's Best Tool for Tomorrow

In today's rapidly evolving world, where technology and information grow unprecedentedly, the ability to think critically is no longer just beneficial—it's essential. This foundational skill helps children adapt, make informed decisions, and solve problems effectively. As the first stepping stone in nurturing these capabilities, understanding why critical thinking is crucial has never been more important. The early childhood years are not just about learning basic skills but are pivotal in shaping how a child interacts with their complex world.

Critical thinking is not innate but a skill that can be nurtured and developed. Early childhood offers a unique window of opportunity to lay the groundwork for this vital skill set. The brain's plasticity during this period makes it the ideal time to start cultivating thinking methods that question, analyze, and assess information. Recognizing the pivotal role of early childhood in developing these skills can transform how we approach education at this sensitive stage.

The impact of embedding critical thinking from a young age is profound. Children equipped with this skill tend to embark on a lifelong journey of learning that is reflective, self-directed, and deeply engaging. Such individuals are better prepared to face the challenges of an interconnected world and possess a keener ability to adapt to change. Exploring the various impacts of critical thinking on a child's development highlights its role in academic success and overall personal and social capability.

This book aims to shift the narrative from why to how—transforming understanding into action. By introducing practical strategies tailored for young learners, parents and educators can start enhancing critical thinking skills in months, not years, without falling prey to the misconception that these concepts are too advanced for young minds.

The core issue addressed here revolves around the common oversight in early education—failing to focus adequately on developing critical thinkers from an early age. The subsequent chapters build on this foundation by offering insights into strategies that nurture preschool-aged children's curiosity, analytical thinking, and creativity.

As readers progress through this guide, they will learn the importance and practical aspects of fostering an environment conducive to intellectual growth. This environment encourages questioning norms, connecting ideas, and expressing thoughts innovatively—all essential ingredients for critical thinkers.

Each chapter will equip you with the knowledge and tools to integrate critical thinking exercises seamlessly into daily interactions with children. These strategies are designed to be effective and engaging, ensuring that they capture the interest of young minds while promoting cognitive development.

Understanding and implementing the concepts discussed here will set a strong foundation for your child's future learning journey, marked by curiosity, resilience, and adaptability. Engaging actively with these strategies will enhance your child's cognitive abilities and empower them as thoughtful individuals ready to tackle the complexities of their ever-changing world.

In today's fast-paced world, the ability to think critically is more crucial than ever before. With technological advancements and an overflow of information, individuals must navigate complex situations, make informed decisions, and solve problems effectively. Critical thinking skills are desirable and necessary for success in various aspects of life.

Understanding the importance of critical thinking is fundamental as it equips individuals with the tools needed to analyze information objectively, assess situations accurately, and make sound judgments. In a rapidly changing world where challenges arise unexpectedly, thinking critically allows individuals to adapt quickly and find innovative solutions to problems. Cultivating these skills early on can lay a strong foundation for future success and resilience in uncertainty.

Moreover, critical thinking goes beyond academic achievements; it is a life skill that enhances communication, fosters creativity, and promotes independent thinking. In a world where opinions are abundant, and misinformation is rampant, individuals with strong critical thinking skills can discern facts from fiction, making them less susceptible to manipulation and more capable of forming well-founded opinions.

As parents or educators, recognizing the significance of critical thinking in today's landscape is pivotal. By instilling these skills in children early on, we empower them to become confident decision-makers, effective problem-solvers, and lifelong learners. Investing in developing critical thinking in young minds sets the stage for a future where individuals can navigate challenges with agility and intelligence.

Unleashing Early Critical Power

Early childhood is critical in laying the foundations for critical thinking skills. During these formative years, children are like sponges, absorbing information and experiences that shape their cognitive development. Parents and educators need to recognize the significance of this period and actively engage children in activities that promote problem-solving, analysis, and decision-making. By fostering a stimulating environment rich in opportunities for exploration and discovery, caregivers can nurture the budding seeds of critical thinking in young minds.

Children are naturally curious and eager to learn from the world around them. Encouraging this innate curiosity through hands-on experiences, open-ended questions, and exposure to diverse perspectives can help cultivate their analytical and reasoning abilities. Simple activities like puzzles, sorting games, or discussions about cause and effect can spark children's interest in understanding how things work and why they happen.

As adults, we must be mindful of our language when interacting with children. Encouraging them to ask questions, voice their opinions, and engage in discussions fosters a sense of confidence in their intellectual capabilities. By creating a safe space to express their thoughts and ideas without fear of judgment, we empower them to think critically and develop their unique perspectives on the world.

Moreover, modeling critical thinking skills ourselves can have a profound impact on children's development. They learn by example when we approach problems thoughtfully, weighing different options and considering consequences. Demonstrating how to navigate challenges with resilience and adaptability instills valuable lessons they can carry into their problem-solving endeavors.

In early childhood education, moving beyond traditional rote learning methods and embracing interactive, engaging, and thought-provoking approaches that stimulate children's cognitive growth is crucial. By integrating critical thinking into everyday activities, such as storytelling, playtime, or nature walks, we seamlessly embed these skills into their learning experiences without overwhelming them with formal instruction.

By recognizing the pivotal role of early childhood in shaping critical thinking foundations, we empower ourselves as caregivers and educators to create an environment where young minds can thrive intellectually. With intentional guidance, support, and opportunities for exploration, we pave the way for children to become agile thinkers who can navigate the complexities of an ever-evolving world with confidence and clarity.

Critical thinking shapes adaptability and problem-solving skills throughout a child's lifelong learning journey. Parents and educators can set children up for success in an ever-evolving world by instilling the foundations of critical thinking early on.

The impacts of nurturing essential thinking abilities are far-reaching, influencing academic performance, future career prospects, and personal growth.

Encouraging Curiosity: One of the key impacts of fostering critical thinking in children is promoting curiosity. When children have the tools to question, analyze, and evaluate information, they become naturally curious about the world around them. This curiosity drives them to seek new knowledge, explore different perspectives, and engage meaningfully with complex problems. By nurturing this innate curiosity, parents and educators can create a lifelong learner eager to discover, innovate, and grow.

Enhanced Problem-Solving Skills: Critical thinking is closely linked to problem-solving abilities. Children with strong critical thinking skills are better equipped to approach challenges systematically and logically. They can break down complex problems into manageable parts, identify underlying issues, and generate creative solutions. These problem-solving skills benefit academic performance and prepare children for real-world scenarios where adaptability and quick thinking are essential.

Empowering Decision-Making: Another significant impact of critical thinking on a child's development is the ability to make informed decisions. Critical thinkers are adept at weighing evidence, considering multiple viewpoints, and evaluating potential outcomes before making a choice. By empowering children with these decision-making skills from an early age, parents and educators help them navigate a world filled with options and consequences. This ability to make informed decisions lays the foundation for responsible behavior and ethical reasoning as children grow into adulthood.

Cultivating Resilience: Critical thinking fosters resilience in children by teaching them how to overcome obstacles and setbacks. When faced with challenges or failures, critical thinkers approach these situations as opportunities for growth rather than insurmountable barriers. Parents and educators empower children to persevere in adversity, learn from their mistakes, and confidently adapt to changing circumstances by cultivating resilience through essential thinking skills.

In essence, the impacts of critical thinking on a child's lifelong learning journey are profound and multifaceted. By nurturing essential thinking skills early on, parents and educators provide children with the tools they need to thrive in an increasingly complex world. From enhancing problem-solving abilities to empowering decision-making and fostering resilience, critical thinking lays the groundwork for success in academics, careers, relationships, and personal development. Embracing the power of critical thinking sets children on a path toward continuous growth, exploration, and discovery throughout their lives.

As we navigate the complexities of today's world, the importance of critical thinking cannot be overstated. This chapter has laid the foundation for understanding why these skills are beneficial and essential for young minds. The rapidly evolving landscape of technology and global interconnectivity demands more than ever that our children not only adapt but also thrive in these changing environments. Focusing on early childhood gives our children the tools to face these challenges with confidence and curiosity.

Critical thinking is more than an academic skill; it's a lifelong asset that influences how a child learns, adapts, and views the world. Initiating this journey early sets the stage for continuous growth and development. It's about preparing them not just for school but for life. The strategies discussed here are designed to be straightforward and actionable, ensuring every child can benefit from them without delay.

The journey through this book promises to be both enlightening and transformative. Each chapter builds on the next, offering practical advice and proven strategies to help you foster a nurturing environment that promotes critical thinking. You hold the key to unlocking your child's potential, and by turning these pages, you're taking a decisive step toward shaping a resilient, thoughtful, and capable individual.

Remember, the role you play in your child's development is irreplaceable. By enhancing their critical thinking abilities, you're guiding them toward academic success and empowering them to navigate life's challenges with agility and insight. Let's embrace this opportunity with enthusiasm and commitment, ensuring our children grow into adults who are thinkers, innovators, and leaders in their own right.

With each chapter of this book, anticipate discovering more about how you can effectively mold the critical thinkers of tomorrow. Here's to embarking on a rewarding adventure that promises significant rewards for you and your child—rewards that extend far beyond the classroom into every aspect of personal and professional life.

Chapter 2: From Theory to Play: Bridging the Gap in Early Education

"Critical thinking is more than just a simple thought process. It involves thinking on a much deeper underlying level rather than just at the surface."

J. Martin

Unleashing the Power of Play: Transform Early Learning Today

Understanding that early childhood is a pivotal stage for developing critical thinking skills is not just academic—it's a practical necessity in today's fast-evolving world. The cognitive abilities of preschool-aged children are often underestimated, yet they possess a remarkable capacity to engage with complex concepts through appropriately designed activities. This understanding forms the cornerstone of effective early education strategies that bridge the gap between developmental theory and playful practice.

The essence of this approach lies in transforming theoretical knowledge into engaging, hands-on experiences that captivate young minds. By incorporating fun, age-appropriate activities, caregivers and educators can significantly enhance children's ability to think critically from a very young age. This chapter delves deep into how to effectively translate cognitive development theories into practical applications that are both enjoyable and educational.

Firstly, it is crucial to grasp the fundamental theories of cognitive development, such as those proposed by Piaget and Vygotsky. These theories provide a framework for understanding how children perceive and interact with their environment at various stages of their growth. For instance, Piaget's stages of cognitive development explain why certain games or activities might be more suitable for children at specific ages or developmental stages.

Following this foundational knowledge, the chapter guides you through creating playful learning activities that align with these developmental theories. It offers detailed instructions on setting up activities that fit the child's developmental stage and intrigue and stimulate their curiosity. Whether through storytelling, problem-solving games, or creative arts, each activity is designed to make learning a dynamic and interactive experience.

Moreover, addressing the challenge of conveying abstract concepts to young learners is another focal point. The chapter provides innovative methods and practical tools that simplify complex ideas, making them accessible and understandable to children. Through hands-on activities like sorting games or simple experiments, abstract concepts are transformed into tangible learning experiences.

Incorporating play into the learning process is not just about keeping children entertained; it's a strategic approach to enhance their learning outcomes. Playful learning strategies such as scavenger hunts or role-playing are discussed extensively, providing various options to incorporate these methods into everyday learning scenarios.

Lastly, reflection on these applications is vital in reinforcing the connection between theory and practice. By encouraging self-reflection and adaptation of strategies to meet individual needs, caregivers can continue to refine their approach to early childhood education.

Step-by-Step Guide: "Playful Minds Framework"

Step 1: Understanding Cognitive Development Theories

Start by familiarizing yourself with critical cognitive development theories. This understanding will guide you in choosing appropriate activities based on children's developmental stages.

Step 2: Translating Theory into Playful Activities

Develop a range of activities that reflect these theories. Ensure these are fun and engaging while promoting critical thinking skills such as analysis, reasoning, and problem-solving.

Step 3: Hands-On Experiences for Abstract Concepts

Introduce abstract concepts through tangible experiences. Use everyday objects and simple experiments to demonstrate complex ideas in a way young children can understand.

Step 4: Incorporating Playful Learning Strategies

Emphasize the importance of play in learning. Utilize various playful strategies that encourage active participation and stimulate critical thinking.

Step 5: Reflecting on Theory-to-Play Connections

Regularly reflect on your practices. Adapt your strategies to suit individual learning styles better and document your observations for continuous improvement.

By following these steps diligently, you're not just teaching; you're opening up a world of wonders where young minds can thrive through exploration and discovery. Each step empowers you to transform theoretical knowledge into practical exercises that foster an environment rich in creativity and critical thinking.

Early childhood educators often find themselves at a crossroads where cognitive development theories meet the reality of engaging young minds. Translating complex theories into practical, fun activities for children can be daunting, but it is crucial for developing critical thinking skills early on. Understanding how young children learn and grow is the first step in creating age-appropriate and intellectually stimulating activities. Caregivers can effectively bridge the gap between theory and practice by incorporating exploration, questioning, and analysis elements into play-based learning experiences.

One key aspect to consider when designing activities for young children is the need for hands-on experiences. Abstract concepts can be challenging for preschoolers to grasp without tangible examples. By providing concrete materials and opportunities for sensory exploration, educators can make theoretical ideas more accessible and engaging for young learners. Tactile experiences help solidify abstract concepts, allowing children to connect theoretical knowledge with real-world applications.

Another essential factor to consider when creating activities for young children is the element of play. Play is the natural language of childhood and a powerful tool for learning. Incorporating playful elements into educational activities can increase engagement and motivation while fostering creativity and problem-solving skills in children. By infusing playfulness into learning experiences, caregivers can make complex theories more approachable and enjoyable for young minds.

Encouraging exploration is another crucial component of designing activities that promote critical thinking in early childhood. Children are naturally curious and inclined to investigate their surroundings. By providing opportunities for open-ended exploration, caregivers can nurture children's innate sense of wonder and encourage them to ask questions, make discoveries, and draw conclusions on their own.

In summary, translating cognitive development theories into fun, age-appropriate activities for children requires a thoughtful blend of hands-on experiences, playful elements, and opportunities for exploration. By understanding how young minds learn best through concrete examples, play-based learning, and open-ended exploration, caregivers can create enriching environments that lay a strong foundation for critical thinking skills in preschool-aged children.

Embracing Hands-On Learning: Practical Resources for Early Childhood Education

The importance of practical resources and hands-on experiences cannot be overstated in early childhood education. These tangible tools serve as bridges that connect abstract concepts to real-world applications, making learning more engaging and effective for young children. By incorporating hands-on activities, caregivers can help children grasp complex ideas concretely and meaningfully.

One key strategy is to use everyday objects as teaching aids. By leveraging items commonly found in a child's environment, educators can make learning relatable and accessible. For instance, using building blocks to demonstrate mathematical concepts or incorporating nature walks to teach scientific principles can enhance a child's understanding through direct experience.

Another effective method is the use of sensory materials. Engaging multiple senses not only makes learning more interactive but also deepens comprehension. Activities like finger painting to explore colors and textures or sensory bins filled with different materials can stimulate a child's cognitive development while providing a fun and immersive learning experience.

Practical resources also play a crucial role in fostering creativity and problem-solving skills. Through open-ended activities encouraging exploration and experimentation, children learn to think critically and find innovative solutions. Tools like puzzles, art supplies, and manipulatives help develop spatial reasoning, fine motor skills, and creativity in young learners.

Hands-on experiences are particularly effective in teaching social-emotional skills. Collaborative projects and group activities promote teamwork, communication, and empathy among children. By engaging in shared tasks, kids learn critical social dynamics and build essential relationship skills for overall development.

By integrating practical resources into early education, caregivers can create a dynamic learning environment that caters to diverse learning styles and abilities. These tools enhance academic knowledge and nurture essential life skills that prepare children for future success. Through hands-on experiences, young learners can cultivate a love for learning, curiosity for the world, and the confidence to tackle challenges with resilience.

The Playful Learning Framework

The Playful Learning Framework is designed to translate cognitive development theories into engaging and effective educational activities for young children. By incorporating critical principles from significant theories such as Piaget's stages of cognitive development and Vygotsky's social development theory, caregivers can create a dynamic learning environment that nurtures critical thinking skills in preschool-aged children. Let's break down the components of this framework to understand how each part contributes to fostering a rich and stimulating educational experience.

Core Principles Application

The first step of the Playful Learning Framework involves identifying and applying the core principles of cognitive development theories. For instance, drawing from Piaget's preoperational stage, caregivers can develop activities that enhance problem-solving skills through symbolic play. Children can engage in storytelling and perspective-taking by creating scenarios for role-playing and imaginative play, fostering their ability to think critically and creatively.

Social Learning Integration

Building on Vygotsky's emphasis on social learning, the framework includes strategies for designing collaborative games that promote language and concept development through interaction. By encouraging activities like puzzle-solving in pairs or group storytelling sessions, caregivers can effectively leverage the zone of proximal development to scaffold learning experiences. This collaborative approach enhances critical thinking skills by providing opportunities for children to learn from their peers and engage in shared problem-solving.

Material Selection and Adaptation

Selecting and adapting materials that align with these activities is crucial to ensuring their effectiveness. Caregivers must choose toys, books, and digital resources that stimulate critical thinking and are appropriate for the early childhood age group. By incorporating diverse materials that cater to different learning styles, caregivers can create inclusive learning experiences that resonate with each child's unique strengths and preferences.

Evaluation Strategies

The Playful Learning Framework also emphasizes the importance of evaluating the effectiveness of these activities in promoting critical thinking. Caregivers are encouraged to observe children during play, collect feedback on their engagement levels, and adjust activities based on outcomes. This iterative process allows caregivers to fine-tune educational experiences to maximize their impact on children's cognitive development.

The Playful Learning Framework provides a structured approach for caregivers to create engaging and effective educational activities supporting young children's critical thinking. By integrating core principles from cognitive development theories, fostering social learning opportunities, selecting appropriate materials, and evaluating outcomes, caregivers can lay a strong foundation for nurturing critical thinking skills in preschool-aged children.

As we have explored, the early years are learning basic skills and layin and transforming cognitive development theories into engaging activities. We equip children with the tools to explore and understand their world. Practical resources and hands-on experiences are essential in making abstract concepts accessible to young minds. These strategies are helpful and crucial for fostering an environment where young learners can thrive.

It's important to remember that each child is unique, and what works for one may not work for another. This diversity in learning styles makes it all the more necessary to have a variety of approaches at your disposal. Engaging children through play and interactive activities does more than entertain; it opens avenues for deeper understanding and retention of knowledge.

Moving forward, take these insights and apply them with confidence. You have the tools to significantly impact the cognitive development of the children in your care. Embrace the role of both educator and guide and watch as your learners grow into curious, thoughtful individuals. Your efforts today are shaping skills and nurturing future innovators and problem solvers.

Remember, the goal is to teach and inspire a continuous love for learning. By incorporating these playful learning strategies, you're addressing current educational needs and setting the stage for lifelong intellectual engagement. Let's make learning a joyous journey that children are eager to embark on daily.

Chapter 3: Thinking Critically About Tomorrow: Connecting Skills with Real Life

> "It is the mark of an educated mind to be able to entertain a thought without accepting it."
>
> **Aristotle**

From Theories to Tangible Tasks: How Can We Make Critical Thinking Accessible to Children?

Bridging the gap between theoretical frameworks of cognitive development and practical, engaging activities for children is not just beneficial—it's essential. As educators, parents, and mentors, our challenge lies in translating sophisticated concepts into experiences that are both accessible and enjoyable for young minds. This journey from abstract to concrete is crucial in nurturing a child's ability to think critically about the world around them.

The significance of critical thinking in early childhood cannot be overstated. It equips children with the problem-solving skills necessary for academic success and everyday decisions. However, the real value lies in making these skills relatable and applicable in their immediate environment. By integrating real-world scenarios into learning experiences, children begin to see the relevance of critical thinking in their daily lives. This approach enhances their understanding and keeps them engaged and curious.

To effectively foster critical thinking, we must employ examples and case studies that resonate with young learners. These examples should be carefully chosen to reflect situations that children might encounter, enhancing their ability to apply learned concepts independently. Through stories, simulations, and role-playing activities, children can explore various outcomes based on different decisions, which sharpens their analytical skills and decision-making abilities.

Another key element is showing practical applications of these skills. When children understand how critical thinking can help them solve problems or make better decisions, they are more likely to value and utilize these skills proactively. Practical demonstrations can range from sorting out conflicts with peers to planning a straightforward project or even managing basic time schedules for their daily routines. Each scenario encourages children to think critically and assess various factors before making decisions.

Moreover, we must create environments where questioning is encouraged and celebrated. Children should feel comfortable questioning the 'why' and 'how' of things around them without fear of being dismissed. This nurtures an inquisitive mindset, which is fundamental to critical thinking. Educators and parents need strategies that support such an environment—ones that offer guidance without providing all the answers too readily.

Lastly, reflection is a powerful tool in reinforcing learning. After engaging in critical thinking tasks, guiding children through a reflection process helps them internalize what they've learned and understand how it applies to other areas of their lives. This could be as simple as discussing what went well in a project, what didn't, and what they could do differently next time.

This approach ensures that critical thinking doesn't remain an abstract skill discussed only within the confines of a classroom but becomes a tangible tool that children carry into every aspect of their lives. By grounding theoretical knowledge in everyday realities, we provide young learners with skills and a transformed perspective—a way of viewing challenges as opportunities to learn and grow.

Incorporating real-world scenarios into teaching critical thinking to young children can significantly enhance their understanding and engagement with the subject. By connecting abstract concepts to tangible examples from everyday life, educators can help children see the relevance and practical applications of critical thinking skills. When children can relate what they are learning to real-life situations, they are more likely to grasp the importance of critical thinking in problem-solving and decision-making.

One effective way to teach children about critical thinking is through interactive activities that mimic real-world scenarios. For instance, setting up a pretend grocery store where children have to calculate prices, make choices based on budgets, and weigh the pros and cons of different purchases can be a fun and educational way to develop critical thinking skills. By immersing children in these hands-on experiences, they can practice logical reasoning, decision-making, and problem-solving in a safe and engaging environment.

Another strategy is to use storytelling as a tool for teaching critical thinking. Narratives with relatable characters facing dilemmas that require critical thinking can capture children's attention and imagination. Encouraging children to think about how the characters in the story could approach challenges differently or solve problems creatively can help them internalize key concepts of critical thinking without feeling overwhelmed by abstract theories.

Integrating real-world examples into lessons can also help children see the practical applications of critical thinking in their daily lives. By discussing how critical thinking skills are used by scientists, inventors, or even fictional heroes in movies or books, educators can inspire children to see themselves as capable problem-solvers who can make a difference in the world.

Enhancing Problem-Solving with Real-Life Examples and Case Studies

Incorporating real-life examples and case studies into learning experiences can significantly enhance children's problem-solving abilities. Connecting abstract concepts to concrete situations enables young learners to grasp complex ideas more effectively. Engaging with practical scenarios helps children see the relevance of critical thinking in their daily lives, making the learning process more meaningful and engaging.

One effective strategy is to present case studies that are relatable and age-appropriate. For example, discussing a scenario where a character must decide can prompt children to think critically about the problem. Encouraging them to analyze the situation, consider different perspectives, and come up with creative solutions fosters their problem-solving skills in a practical context.

Examples from familiar settings can also aid in connecting theoretical knowledge with real-world applications. Whether it's a story about sharing toys with friends or solving a puzzle, these simple yet impactful examples can help children understand how critical thinking plays out in everyday situations. By showing children that critical thinking is not just a concept but a valuable skill they use regularly, we empower them to engage more actively in learning.

Interactive activities that involve problem-solving based on real-life scenarios can deepen children's understanding of critical thinking. For instance, setting up challenges where they must work together to overcome obstacles or make decisions can hone their analytical skills while promoting collaboration and communication. These hands-on experiences solidify the connection between theory and practice, making abstract ideas more tangible for young minds.

By integrating examples and case studies into learning experiences, we provide children with the tools to navigate challenges and make informed decisions. This approach enhances their problem-solving abilities and cultivates a mindset that values critical thinking as an essential skill for success. Empowering children with practical applications of critical thinking sets them on a path toward becoming confident, resourceful individuals capable of tackling any situation.

In helping children understand the practical applications of critical thinking in their daily lives, it is essential to provide them with opportunities that bridge theoretical concepts with real-world scenarios. One effective strategy is to engage children in problem-solving activities that mimic situations they might encounter in their everyday experiences. For example, presenting them with puzzles or challenges that require logical reasoning and critical analysis can help them see the relevance of these skills outside the classroom.

Integrating critical thinking into daily routines can also be a powerful way to show children how these skills are valuable in their lives. Encouraging them to ask questions, evaluate information, and make informed decisions about simple tasks like organizing toys or planning a playdate can lay the groundwork for more complex problem-solving abilities. By highlighting how critical thinking enhances their ability to navigate everyday situations, children can begin to see its practical significance.

Another strategy is incorporating storytelling into learning experiences to illustrate how critical thinking can lead to creative solutions. By sharing narratives where characters face dilemmas that require thoughtful decision-making, children can vicariously engage in problem-solving and see the positive outcomes of applying critical thinking skills. This approach fosters imagination and demonstrates the real-world impact of logical reasoning and analytical thinking.

Encouraging children to explore different perspectives is crucial in developing their critical thinking abilities. By exposing them to diverse viewpoints through discussions, reading materials, or interactions with others, children learn to consider alternative ideas and evaluate information critically. This practice helps them understand that there are multiple ways to approach a problem and instills a sense of open-mindedness essential for practical critical thinking.

Moreover, engaging children in hands-on activities that require experimentation and exploration can help them develop problem-solving skills organically. Constructing simple machines, conducting science experiments, or participating in group projects can foster teamwork, creativity, and analytical thinking—all essential components of critical thinking. Providing children with opportunities to apply theoretical knowledge in practical settings enhances their understanding of complex concepts and reinforces the value of critical thinking skills.

In guiding children toward recognizing the practical applications of critical thinking in their daily lives, it is crucial to celebrate their successes and efforts along the way. By acknowledging their achievements and growth in problem-solving abilities, children feel motivated to continue honing their critical thinking skills. Creating a supportive environment where mistakes are viewed as learning opportunities fosters resilience and perseverance—a vital mindset for developing critical, solid thinkers.

By implementing these strategies consistently and offering children a variety of engaging experiences that emphasize critical thinking, parents, and educators can empower young learners to see the relevance of these skills in their daily lives. Through hands-on activities, real-world scenarios, storytelling, diverse perspectives, and positive reinforcement, children can develop a strong foundation for critical thinking that will serve them well as they navigate challenges and opportunities in the future.

Bridging Theory to Practice

The journey of teaching young children to think critically is both necessary and rewarding. By integrating real-world scenarios, case studies, and practical applications into their learning experiences, we equip them with the skills to tackle the challenges of tomorrow. This approach makes abstract concepts tangible and instills a lifelong love for learning and problem-solving.

Children learn best when they can see the relevance of their lessons in everyday life. We've discussed various strategies to highlight this relevance, from using simple examples they encounter daily to engaging them in activities that mimic real-life situations. These methods help demystify the process of critical thinking, making it accessible and engaging for young minds.

Encouragement and support are vital components in this educational journey. As educators, parents, or guardians, our role extends beyond mere instruction. It involves being a guide who fosters curiosity and encourages exploration. Your understanding of each child's unique learning style is crucial. Tailoring your approach to meet their needs will enhance their learning experience and boost their confidence and critical thinking capabilities.

Taking Action

To move forward effectively, focus on creating learning moments that invite curiosity and challenging conventional thinking. Encourage questions, foster dialogue, and provide opportunities for children to test their ideas in safe environments. This active participation cements the skills they're developing and shows them the impact of their thoughts and decisions.

Remember, every child has the potential to think critically with the proper guidance and opportunities. By proactively applying the strategies discussed, you play a pivotal role in nurturing this essential skill set. Engage with these young minds actively and watch as they grow into thoughtful, analytical individuals capable of changing the world around them.

Let's continue this journey together, supporting each other as we unlock the incredible potential within each child. The tools and strategies you've learned here are just the beginning. As you implement these ideas, you'll see firsthand how effective they can be in shaping capable, independent thinkers ready to face the future confidently.

Chapter 4: Digitally Wired to Think: Leveraging Technology for Critical Minds

"The function of education is to teach one to think intensively and to think critically. Intelligence plus character – that is the goal of true education."

Martin Luther King Jr.

Harnessing Digital Tools to Cultivate Young Critical Thinkers

In an era where technology is as natural to children as breathing, it's crucial to guide their interactions with digital tools in a way that enhances their critical thinking skills. This chapter delves into the practical application of technology as a pivotal component in developing young minds. Parents and educators can transform everyday tech experiences into profound learning opportunities by carefully selecting and using digital resources.

Digital literacy is not just about understanding how to use technology but about leveraging it to enhance cognitive skills. Evaluating digital tools and apps isn't just about checking age-appropriateness or educational content and how these tools can foster critical thinking. For instance, apps that simulate problem-solving scenarios or allow children to explore cause-and-effect relationships can be incredibly beneficial. These digital environments provide a safe space for children to experiment, make decisions, and see their choices' outcomes, enhancing their analytical skills.

However, integrating technology into learning isn't without challenges. The key is effectively incorporating interactive technology resources without leading to cognitive overload. Children's engagement with digital tools should be balanced and purposeful. Interactive e-books, educational games, and apps designed with input from developmental psychologists can provide engaging, not overwhelming stimuli. It's about creating an ecosystem where technology supports learning in a structured way.

Understanding the balance between screen time and hands-on learning is critical in nurturing well-rounded individuals. While digital tools can offer interactive and engaging ways to develop critical thinking, they cannot wholly replace the tactile experiences of physical interactions with the world. Activities like building blocks, board games, and science experiments provide essential hands-on experiences that develop spatial reasoning, physical coordination, and real-world problem-solving skills.

To implement this balanced approach effectively, caregivers must become adept at choosing the right moments for digital learning and when to encourage offline exploration. For example, using an app that teaches mathematical concepts can be followed by a physical game that utilizes those same concepts. This not only reinforces learning but also helps children make connections between digital inputs and real-world applications.

Moreover, educating children on using technology responsibly is as important as the content they interact with. Discussions about the purpose of each tool and how it fits into their larger learning goals can help make technology use more intentional and meaningful.

We aim to educate and inspire young learners through this strategic approach to technology integration. By presenting them with challenges that require digital and hands-on problem-solving, we prepare them for a world where digital literacy goes hand-in-hand with critical thinking.

By embracing these strategies, caregivers can ensure that children consume digital content and interact with it in ways that build their capacity for critical analysis and thoughtful interaction. The goal is clear: foster a generation of thinkers who are as comfortable with a touchscreen as they are with a conversation, able to navigate an increasingly complex world with confidence and curiosity.

In today's digital age, children are surrounded by technology from a very young age. While some may see this as a cause for concern, it can also be an opportunity to leverage digital tools and apps to enhance critical thinking in young learners. Evaluating these resources is crucial to ensure that they align with educational goals and promote the development of essential skills.

When selecting digital tools and apps for children, it is essential to prioritize those that encourage problem-solving, reasoning, and creativity. Look for applications that present challenges and puzzles, requiring the child to think critically to find solutions. Interactive platforms that engage children in decision-making can foster independence and analytical thinking.

Furthermore, consider the level of scaffolding provided by the tool. Scaffolding refers to the support structures in place to guide children through tasks. Opt for apps that offer gradual difficulty levels, allowing children to build upon their skills progressively. This approach promotes a sense of accomplishment and motivates continued engagement with the material.

Seek out tools that promote collaboration and communication among young learners. Platforms encouraging teamwork and discussion can enhance critical thinking by exposing children to diverse perspectives and ideas. Interactive activities that require group problem-solving can help children develop their analytical skills in a social context.

In addition to fostering critical thinking skills, digital tools should also be age-appropriate. When selecting apps, consider the child's developmental stage and ensure that the content suits their cognitive abilities. Avoid overwhelming young learners with complex tasks or concepts beyond their grasp, as this can lead to frustration rather than productive learning experiences.

Regularly monitor your child's engagement with the tools when evaluating digital resources for critical thinking enhancement. Observe how they interact with the content and assess whether they are challenged appropriately. Please adjust the selection of apps based on your child's progress to ensure continued growth in their critical thinking abilities.

Leveraging Interactive Technology for Critical Thinking in Early Education

Incorporating interactive technology resources into educational activities for young learners can be a powerful tool in fostering critical thinking skills. Technology can potentially engage children in learning through interactive and stimulating activities, making complex concepts more accessible and enjoyable. Digital tools can enhance children's problem-solving abilities, creativity, and analytical thinking when used strategically. By integrating technology into educational settings, caregivers can create dynamic learning environments that cater to diverse learning styles.

One key strategy is to select age-appropriate digital tools that align with the child's developmental stage and educational objectives. Choosing apps and programs that offer interactive challenges, puzzles, or simulations can help children develop critical thinking skills while having fun. It is essential to balance screen time and hands-on activities, ensuring that technology complements rather than replaces traditional learning methods.

Engaging children in collaborative digital activities can also promote critical thinking. By working together on solving problems or completing tasks using technology, children learn how to communicate effectively, consider different perspectives, and brainstorm solutions collectively. Encouraging teamwork through digital platforms can nurture essential skills like collaboration, communication, and critical analysis.

Another effective strategy is to provide guidance and support during technology-based activities. Caregivers can offer prompts, ask open-ended questions, and encourage children to explain their thought processes while using digital tools. This approach helps children develop metacognitive skills, enabling them to reflect on their thinking and problem-solving strategies. By guiding children through technology for learning, caregivers can scaffold their development of critical thinking skills.

It is crucial to monitor and evaluate the impact of technology on children's critical thinking abilities. Observing how children engage with digital tools, identifying areas for improvement, and adjusting the learning experiences accordingly can optimize the benefits of technology in fostering critical thinking. Regular assessment of children's progress and feedback on their use of technology can guide caregivers in tailoring educational activities to enhance critical thinking skills effectively.

Carefully incorporating interactive technology resources into educational activities, caregivers can create enriching learning experiences that stimulate children's critical thinking abilities. Strategic selection of age-appropriate tools, promoting collaboration, providing guidance during activities, and monitoring progress are crucial in leveraging technology to develop young learners' critical minds.

In early childhood education, finding the delicate balance between screen time and hands-on learning is crucial for developing critical thinking skills in young minds. While digital tools and interactive resources can enhance cognitive abilities, it is essential also to prioritize tactile experiences that engage children in physical exploration and problem-solving. Screen time should complement, not replace, hands-on activities that stimulate creativity and critical thinking.

Limiting screen time to allow for ample hands-on learning opportunities is a practical strategy to ensure a well-rounded development of critical thinking skills. Excessive exposure to screens can hinder a child's ability to engage with their environment actively. Encouraging physical play, outdoor activities, and interactive experiments fosters curiosity and problem-solving skills in a more tangible way than digital interactions alone.

Engage children in activities that require them to think critically and solve real-world problems, both on-screen and off. Encouraging them to participate in puzzles, board games, science experiments, or art projects can provide diverse opportunities for applying critical thinking skills outside of digital interfaces. Hands-on experiences help children develop spatial awareness, motor skills, and logical reasoning, essential components of critical thinking.

Use screen time strategically by selecting educational apps and games promoting problem-solving and analytical thinking. Choose applications that encourage creative exploration, strategic planning, and decision-making rather than passive content consumption. Engaging with high-quality digital resources can supplement hands-on learning by providing additional avenues for intellectual growth.

Incorporating a variety of learning modalities—both digital and tactile—allows children to build a robust foundation in critical thinking skills. By striking a balance between screen time activities that challenge cognitive abilities and hands-on experiences that nurture physical interaction and creativity, caregivers can create an enriching environment for young learners. Remember that moderation is vital; optimizing the blend of technology with traditional learning methods can maximize both benefits.

In our exploration of how to best utilize technology for fostering critical thinking in young learners, we've seen the importance of carefully selecting digital tools that are both engaging and educational. The key is not just to integrate technology into learning environments but to do so in a way that enhances cognitive development without causing overload. This balance ensures that children remain curious and motivated while developing essential problem-solving skills.

Technology should be a bridge, not a barrier, to critical thinking. Educators and parents can create opportunities for children to apply their learning in meaningful contexts by choosing appropriate apps and digital resources. This real-world application is crucial because it shows children the practical impact of their thoughts and decisions, making the learning process relevant and exciting.

Furthermore, understanding the balance between screen time and hands-on learning is vital. Too much screen time can lead to passive consumption rather than active learning. Conversely, well-integrated technology can stimulate an interactive learning experience that encourages more profound engagement with the material. It's about making intelligent choices that align with developmental goals.

Encourage autonomy in young learners by allowing them to navigate these technologies under guidance. This boosts their confidence and enhances their decision-making skills as they discern what tools best meet their learning needs.

By implementing these strategies, we equip children to think critically and apply these skills fluidly across various aspects of their lives. Let's empower our young learners with the right tools and guidance to unlock their potential in a digitally enriched world.

Chapter 5: Learning Unleashed: Embracing Diversity in Critical Education

"Thinking is the hardest work there is, which is the probable reason why so few engage in it."

Henry Ford

Harness the Power of Technology in Early Childhood Education

In an era of ubiquitous digital tools, their potential to foster critical thinking in young learners is immense and largely untapped. This insight explores how digital apps and resources can be creatively deployed to cater to diverse learning styles and needs, enhancing early childhood cognitive development.

Understanding the diversity of learning styles is crucial. Every child absorbs and processes information differently—some visually, others through auditory, and others through kinesthetic methods. Digital tools offer versatile approaches that can be customized to fit these varying needs effectively. For example, interactive story apps can benefit visual learners with vibrant animations, while auditory learners might thrive with storytelling podcasts designed for children.

The next step is discovering inclusive teaching strategies that accommodate and actively engage all children. Interactive digital platforms allow for adaptability in lesson plans so that teachers can offer a variety of content delivery methods simultaneously. This keeps all students engaged and encourages them to develop critical thinking skills by effectively interacting with the material.

It's also imperative to address individual strengths and weaknesses in educational planning. Digital tools provide an excellent opportunity for personalized learning experiences. Adaptive learning software, which adjusts the difficulty level of tasks based on the learner's performance, ensures that each child is challenged just enough to foster growth without causing frustration or disengagement.

Integrating technology in education offers more than just convenience; it introduces a dynamic element to learning that traditional methods might lack. By leveraging apps and online resources, educators can create a rich, interactive learning environment that encourages children to question, analyze, and think critically from a young age.

Moreover, technology in education supports educators by providing them with data-driven insights into each student's progress. This information is crucial for developing targeted interventions that help bridge learning gaps and enhance each student's critical thinking capabilities.

To make the most out of digital educational tools, parents and educators must choose apps and resources specifically designed to develop analytical skills and problem-solving abilities. Resources should be evaluated for their content quality and ability to engage students in higher-order thinking processes.

By embracing the diverse capabilities of digital tools in early education, we can create a foundation for lifelong learning where every child can fully develop their potential. This approach not only makes learning more accessible and engaging but also prepares young minds to navigate a complex world with confidence and creativity.

In early childhood education, understanding how to tailor learning experiences to diverse learning styles and needs is paramount to fostering critical thinking skills in young minds. Every child has unique strengths, weaknesses, and preferences when absorbing information and engaging with educational content. Recognizing and embracing this diversity is the first step towards creating a rich learning environment that nurtures critical thinking abilities effectively.

By acknowledging and accommodating diverse learning styles, educators and parents can create a more inclusive and engaging educational experience for children. Some children may thrive in visual environments, while others may excel with auditory or kinesthetic learning methods. Tailoring lessons to incorporate various modes of instruction can help cater to a broader range of learners, ensuring that no child is left behind in the quest to develop critical thinking skills.

Flexibility in teaching methods is critical. Offering a mix of activities that appeal to different learning styles can enhance comprehension and stimulate curiosity and creativity in young learners. For instance, incorporating hands-on experiments for kinesthetic learners or visual aids for visual learners can make complex concepts more accessible and enjoyable for all children.

Individualized attention is crucial. Each child has their own pace of learning and unique areas where they may struggle or excel. Taking the time to understand these individual differences allows educators and parents to tailor educational approaches accordingly. By addressing these specific needs, children are better equipped to develop their critical thinking abilities organically.

Cultivating Critical Thinkers through Inclusive Teaching Strategies

In fostering critical thinking skills in children, employing inclusive teaching strategies that cater to diverse learning styles and needs is crucial. Understanding that each child has unique strengths and challenges is the first step toward creating an environment where all students can thrive. By acknowledging and embracing this diversity, educators can tailor their teaching methods to ensure that every child has the opportunity to develop their critical thinking abilities.

One effective strategy is differentiation, which involves modifying lessons and activities to accommodate various learning preferences. Educators can engage students with different learning styles by incorporating visual, auditory, and kinesthetic elements into lessons. For instance, multimedia presentations, hands-on experiments, and group discussions can provide a well-rounded approach that caters to various preferences.

Another valuable approach is promoting collaborative learning, where students work together on projects and tasks. This encourages teamwork and communication skills and exposes children to different perspectives and ways of thinking. Educators can create an inclusive environment where all voices are heard by fostering community within the classroom.

Incorporating technology into the curriculum can also be a powerful tool for promoting critical thinking skills in children. Educational apps and online resources offer interactive experiences that can engage students in problem-solving activities and creative thinking exercises. By leveraging digital tools that adapt to individual learning needs, educators can provide personalized learning experiences that cater to each child's strengths and weaknesses.

Encouraging open-ended questions during discussions and assignments can also stimulate critical thinking in children. Instead of seeking one correct answer, these questions prompt students to explore various possibilities, analyze information critically, and articulate their reasoning. By fostering a culture of inquiry and curiosity, educators can instill a lifelong love of learning in their students.

Overall, embracing diversity in education requires a commitment to understanding and supporting each child's unique journey toward developing critical thinking skills. Educators can create a dynamic learning environment where all children can thrive academically and personally by implementing inclusive teaching strategies, leveraging technology effectively, promoting collaboration, and encouraging inquiry.

Addressing individual strengths and weaknesses in learning plans is crucial to fostering critical thinking skills in children. Every child is unique, with their abilities and areas for improvement. Recognizing and tailoring educational strategies to cater to these differences can significantly impact a child's cognitive development.

Identifying a child's strengths allows educators and parents to build on what the child excels at, providing opportunities for them to shine and feel confident in their abilities. Whether a child shows exceptional creativity, problem-solving skills, or communication prowess, leveraging these strengths can enhance their learning experience.

On the other hand, acknowledging weaknesses is equally important. Educators can provide targeted support and resources to help them overcome obstacles by pinpointing areas where a child may struggle. This personalized approach boosts the child's confidence and fosters resilience and a growth mindset.

Creating individualized learning plans based on a child's unique profile involves a combination of observation, assessment, and ongoing feedback. Regular check-ins with the child can help gauge their progress and adjust teaching methods to ensure optimal growth.

Incorporating varied teaching techniques tailored to address specific strengths and weaknesses can make learning more engaging and effective. For example, visual learners may benefit from colorful diagrams and infographics, while kinesthetic learners may thrive through hands-on activities and experiments.

Embracing diversity in learning plans also means being open to alternative approaches that cater to different learning styles. Flexibility in teaching methods allows for a more inclusive educational environment where all children can excel based on their preferences.

Celebrating progress and small victories motivates children to continue challenging themselves and pushing their boundaries. A positive attitude towards successes and setbacks nurtures a resilient mindset essential for developing critical thinking skills.

Embracing diversity in education is a necessary and powerful tool to foster critical thinking from an early age. By tailoring educational approaches to meet diverse learning styles and needs, we ensure that every child has the opportunity to thrive. Incorporating digital tools and interactive apps plays a crucial role in this modern educational landscape, engaging children in ways that resonate with their individual experiences and spark their curiosity.

Educators and parents alike must focus on inclusivity. This means deploying teaching strategies that are not only accessible but also adaptable to various strengths and weaknesses. Each child's unique potential can be unlocked when they feel supported and understood in their learning environment. It's about making each student feel valued, which fuels their desire to explore and understand the world around them.

The importance of recognizing individual strengths and weaknesses cannot be overstated. It empowers educators to craft learning experiences that are not only educational but also profoundly resonant with each child. By addressing these individual traits, we build trust and encouragement, which is essential for fostering an atmosphere where critical thinking can flourish.

Action is key. Encourage the use of educational apps and tools that promote critical thinking. These resources should be considered companions in the learning journey, chosen thoughtfully to align with educational goals emphasizing essential analysis and creative problem-solving.

Moving forward, let's commit to these adaptive, inclusive strategies that respect and celebrate the diversity of learners. By doing so, we not only enhance the educational outcomes for children but also prepare them to navigate a complex world with confidence and competence. Let's take these steps together, continually adapting and improving our methods to meet the needs of every young learner.

Chapter 6: Every Day, Every Way: Integrating Critical Thought into Life

"To think critically, you have to be both analytical and motivated."

Carol Dweck

Transforming Everyday Moments into Opportunities for Growth

In early childhood development, tailoring educational approaches to meet diverse learning needs isn't just beneficial—it's essential. Every child possesses unique abilities and preferences that shape their perception and interaction with the world. By embracing these differences, caregivers and educators can craft learning environments that foster critical thinking, creativity, and resilience. This chapter integrates critical thought into daily activities, ensuring every child participates and thrives.

Understanding that each child learns differently is the first step toward cultivating an inclusive educational setting. Traditional one-size-fits-all teaching methods often overlook the nuanced needs of individual learners, which can stifle potential and discourage engagement. Instead, by observing and recognizing how each child absorbs information best—be it through visual aids, hands-on activities, or auditory instructions—caregivers can adapt their strategies to optimize learning outcomes.

Implementing holistic approaches to embed critical thinking into daily routines is more than a teaching strategy; it's a way of life. For example, simple activities like meal preparation or story time can be transformed into critical thinking exercises. Questions such as "What do you think will happen next?" or "Why do you think this ingredient is important?" encourage children to analyze situations and anticipate outcomes, nurturing a habit of inquiry.

Moreover, continuous problem-solving challenges keep the mind agile and build endurance when facing difficulties. Introducing varied scenarios that require different thinking strategies helps children learn to adapt and apply their knowledge flexibly. This is crucial in developing resilience—an ability that will benefit them throughout their lives.

Creating a culture of inquiry and analysis involves more than just asking questions; it requires a supportive atmosphere where children feel valued and understood. This environment encourages them to express their thoughts without fear of judgment, fostering an open dialogue that promotes more profound understanding and respect for diverse perspectives.

Finally, integrating critical thinking into everyday activities should be seen as an ongoing journey rather than a destination. Each day presents new opportunities for exploration and growth for children and their caregivers. By committing to this continual process of learning and adaptation, caregivers can ensure that children learn about the world and how to think about it critically.

Through these strategies, we address our young learners' immediate educational needs and lay a foundation for lifelong learning and problem-solving capabilities. The goal is clear: to prepare children for school and life.

Incorporating critical thinking into daily learning routines is fundamental in shaping young minds for a world of wonders. By infusing everyday activities with opportunities for analysis, problem-solving, and creativity, caregivers can create an environment that nurtures cognitive development and fosters resilience in children. One holistic approach to embedding critical thinking skills involves integrating thought-provoking questions into routine tasks, encouraging children to explore multiple perspectives and solutions.

Engaging in open-ended discussions during activities like meal times or walks can stimulate critical thinking by prompting children to articulate their thoughts, express opinions, and consider alternative viewpoints. Encouraging them to question the world around them fosters curiosity and analytical thinking, laying a solid foundation for future learning.

Games and puzzles that require strategic thinking or problem-solving can also effectively integrate critical thought into daily life. Activities like building blocks, board games, or scavenger hunts challenge children to think creatively and adapt their strategies based on the situation. This valuable skill set extends beyond the game itself.

By incorporating critical thinking into everyday interactions, caregivers help children develop a natural inclination towards questioning, analyzing, and evaluating information—a crucial ability in navigating an increasingly complex world. Consistency is vital; reinforcing these skills through regular practice ensures that critical thinking becomes a habitual part of a child's learning journey.

Fostering Creativity, Flexibility, and Resilience in Critical Thinking Skills

Creativity, flexibility, and resilience are paramount in nurturing critical thinking skills in young minds. Caregivers can enhance their cognitive abilities by providing continuous challenges and encouraging children to think outside the box. Creativity shapes how children approach problem-solving, enabling them to explore multiple perspectives and innovative solutions. Flexibility equips them with the adaptability to navigate complex situations and confidently embrace change. On the other hand, resilience instills the determination to persevere through challenges and setbacks, fostering a growth mindset essential for lifelong learning.

One effective method to cultivate these traits is engaging children in varied problem-solving tasks requiring them to think critically and creatively. By presenting open-ended questions or scenarios that prompt imaginative responses, caregivers can stimulate children's curiosity and encourage them to explore different possibilities. Encouraging experimentation and allowing room for trial and error empowers children to take risks in their thinking, leading to valuable learning experiences that promote growth.

Continuous exposure to diverse challenges further reinforces these skills, as regular practice is critical to mastering any skill. Introducing puzzles, riddles, or brain teasers into daily routines can allow children to apply critical thinking in a fun and engaging manner. Additionally, incorporating role-playing activities or creative projects enables them to exercise their problem-solving abilities in a more interactive setting, enhancing cognitive and social skills.

Creating an environment that values exploration and curiosity fosters creativity and flexibility. Encouraging children to ask questions, explore new ideas, and think independently nurtures their innate sense of wonder and imagination. Caregivers empower children to embrace their unique perspectives and develop confidence in their creative abilities by providing a safe space for experimentation and self-expression.

In fostering critical thinking skills in children, creating a culture of inquiry and analysis in everyday activities is paramount. By integrating these practices into daily routines, caregivers can naturally encourage young minds to question, explore, and evaluate information. Encouraging curiosity and nurturing a sense of wonder through simple activities like asking open-ended questions, exploring new environments, or discussing various perspectives on familiar topics can lay the foundation for lifelong critical thinking skills.

Modeling critical thinking behaviors is vital in creating a culture of inquiry. Children learn by observing those around them, so caregivers should demonstrate how to approach problems analytically, consider different viewpoints, and seek evidence to support conclusions. Engaging children in discussions that require them to justify their opinions or think critically about cause-and-effect relationships can further reinforce these skills. Caregivers can cultivate an environment where curiosity and questioning are celebrated by making critical thinking a visible and valued part of daily interactions.

Integrating analysis into playtime is another effective way to foster critical thinking skills. Simple games like puzzles, building blocks, or scavenger hunts can challenge children to think creatively, problem-solve, and strategize. Caregivers can also introduce planning, decision-making, and reflection activities to encourage children to think ahead and evaluate outcomes. Creating opportunities for experimentation allows children to test hypotheses, learn from mistakes, and refine their problem-solving strategies in a supportive environment.

Emphasizing the importance of evidence-based reasoning is crucial in nurturing critical thinking skills. Encouraging children to ask for reasons behind statements or beliefs helps them develop a healthy skepticism and the ability to discern reliable information from opinions or assumptions. Caregivers can guide children in seeking evidence from reliable sources, analyzing data objectively, and drawing logical conclusions based on facts rather than emotions or biases.

Incorporating real-world scenarios into everyday conversations can help children apply critical thinking skills to practical situations. Discussing current events, ethical dilemmas, or dilemmas encountered in daily life encourages children to consider multiple perspectives, weigh the consequences, and make informed decisions. By connecting critical thinking to real-life experiences, caregivers help children understand the relevance and impact of these skills beyond academic settings.

By creating a culture of inquiry and analysis in everyday activities, caregivers nurture critical thinking skills and promote a mindset of continuous learning and growth. Encouraging children to question, explore, analyze, and reflect empowers them to navigate an increasingly complex world with confidence and resilience. By embedding critical thinking into daily interactions, caregivers provide children with essential tools for success in both academic pursuits and personal development.

Integrating critical thought into daily routines is beneficial and essential for nurturing young minds adept at navigating a complex world. By tailoring educational approaches to meet the diverse learning needs of children, we empower them to develop crucial skills such as creativity, flexibility, and resilience. Remember, every child has unique strengths and preferences, and recognizing these can significantly enhance learning effectiveness.

Practical Strategies

To make the integration of critical thinking seamless and effective, consider practical strategies that can be easily incorporated into everyday activities. For instance, encouraging children to ask questions and explore various outcomes in simple scenarios like choosing a book or planning a small project can foster a culture of inquiry. This approach doesn't require extensive resources but rather a shift in how we perceive and respond to children's curiosity.

Continuous Challenges

It's also vital to provide continuous challenges that push the boundaries of a child's comfort zone. This doesn't mean overwhelming them but offering incrementally more complex challenges based on their abilities. Such challenges keep the mind engaged and build resilience over time, essential for academic and personal growth.

Culture of Inquiry

Creating a culture of inquiry within everyday interactions lays a foundation for lifelong learning and critical analysis. This culture encourages an accumulation of knowledge, deep understanding, and the ability to apply knowledge in varied situations. Whether through discussions at the dinner table or during playtime, every moment holds potential for critical engagement.

The effort to integrate critical thinking into daily life with children is indeed an investment in their future capabilities. As caregivers and educators, adopting these strategies ensures we address immediate educational needs and prepare young minds to successfully navigate an increasingly complex world.

By taking these steps today, we set the stage for a generation that thinks critically and approaches the world with an analytical mind ready to tackle any challenge. Let's commit to these practices, ensuring our young learners become capable, confident adults.

Chapter 7: Tracking the Thinker: Measuring Critical Progress

"Critical thinking is the intellectual engine

of a functional democracy."

Noam Chomsky

Unveiling the Blueprint: A Strategic Approach to Cultivating Young Critical Thinkers

In a world teeming with information and ever-evolving challenges, equipping children with robust critical thinking skills is more than a necessity—it's a priority. This chapter delves deeply into how caregivers and educators can assess and enhance critical thinking in young learners, setting a foundation that transcends academic success and fosters a lifelong passion for inquiry and problem-solving.

Understanding the significance of assessing critical thinking development is paramount. It's not merely about recognizing whether a child can distinguish between red and blue or choose the correct shape that fits the puzzle. It's about discerning how they approach these decisions. Do they show curiosity? Can they explain their choices? Assessing these skills helps pinpoint strengths and areas needing bolstering, enabling targeted interventions that cultivate deeper intellectual engagement.

Implementing diverse evaluation methods forms the core of our strategic approach. Observational techniques, questioning methodologies, and portfolio assessments are a few tools at our disposal. Each technique offers unique insights into a child's thinking processes, providing a multi-faceted picture of their cognitive development. However, the utility of these methods extends beyond mere assessment; they are integral in shaping customized learning experiences that resonate with each child's developmental stage and learning style.

Documenting progress is as crucial as the evaluation itself. Adequate documentation captures the milestones reached and the nuanced journey along the way. Utilizing digital platforms for real-time tracking or maintaining physical portfolios can streamline this process, ensuring no critical insight into a child's cognitive growth is overlooked.

Setting Milestones: Navigating the Journey of Cognitive Growth

When charting the course of a child's cognitive development, setting realistic milestones is essential. These milestones act as checkpoints that guide educators and parents in recognizing significant achievements and adjusting strategies as needed. They should reflect both the developmental norms of early childhood and be tailored to each child's unique pace of learning.

Celebrating achievements reinforces the value of effort and resilience in young learners. Whether through recognition certificates or simple family gatherings to acknowledge milestones, these celebrations boost confidence and encourage children to set new goals. More importantly, involving children in reflecting on their progress fosters self-awareness and motivation—critical drivers in lifelong learning.

Crafting Critical Thinkers: A Step-by-Step Guide

Step 1: Grasping Significance

Begin by understanding why we assess critical thinking skills.

Recognize patterns in cognitive strengths and weaknesses to tailor educational approaches effectively.

Step 2: Methods in Action

Explore various evaluation methods like observational checklists, interactive questioning, or creative portfolios. Implement them thoughtfully, considering each child's individuality.

Step 3: Keeping Track

Document each step of your young learner's critical thinking journey. Use accessible tools—digital or analog—to record observations systematically.

Step 4: Milestone Mapping

Set achievable goals tailored to your child's developmental stage and individual capabilities. Regularly review these milestones for any necessary adjustments.

Step 5: Celebrate Growth

Acknowledge every achievement, big or small. Engage in meaningful celebrations, encouraging reflection on personal growth and setting the stage for future learning endeavors.

By meticulously tracking and fostering critical thinking early, we enhance academic readiness and empower children to navigate life with resilience and creativity. This holistic approach ensures that today's young learners transform into tomorrow's visionary thinkers ready to face any challenge confidently.

Assessing and monitoring the development of critical thinking skills in early childhood is crucial to nurturing young minds for future success. Understanding the significance of evaluating a child's progress in critical thinking allows caregivers to tailor their educational approach effectively. By actively tracking and measuring critical thinking development, caregivers can identify strengths and areas for improvement and adjust their strategies accordingly. This proactive approach ensures that children receive the necessary support and guidance to improve their cognitive growth.

One key benefit of assessing critical thinking skills is identifying cognitive strengths. Through observation and evaluation, caregivers can pinpoint areas where a child excels in critical thinking. Recognizing these strengths allows caregivers to provide enrichment activities that further enhance the child's abilities, fostering a deep appreciation for complex problem-solving and analysis.

On the flip side, monitoring critical thinking development also highlights areas that require attention. Identifying gaps or challenges in a child's critical thinking skills enables caregivers to implement targeted interventions to support growth and improvement. By addressing these areas early on, caregivers can prevent potential learning obstacles from becoming significant barriers to a child's academic success.

Moreover, regular assessment of critical thinking skills provides caregivers insight into a child's learning progress. Tracking developmental milestones and observing changes in a child's approach to problem-solving offers valuable information on their cognitive growth trajectory. This data-driven approach empowers caregivers to make informed decisions about educational strategies and interventions tailored to each child's needs.

By understanding the significance of assessing and monitoring critical thinking development, caregivers can create a supportive environment that nurtures cognitive growth. Emphasizing the importance of ongoing evaluation ensures that children receive the individualized attention necessary to thrive academically and personally. Carefully tracking critical thinking progress, caregivers lay a strong foundation for lifelong learning and success.

Evaluating Critical Thinking Progress in Early Childhood Education

Now that we understand the importance of tracking critical thinking progress in early childhood education, it's time to delve into practical methods for evaluating and documenting a child's development in this crucial area. By implementing various evaluation techniques, caregivers can gain valuable insights into a child's critical thinking skills and tailor their approach to nurture these abilities further.

One effective method is observation. Caregivers can gather valuable information about their critical thinking processes by keenly observing a child during play, problem-solving activities, or interactions with others. Noting how a child approaches challenges, solves problems, and communicates ideas provides rich data for assessing their cognitive development.

Engaging in dialogue with the child is another powerful evaluation tool. Caregivers can assess the depth of a child's reasoning, logic, and creativity by asking open-ended questions and encouraging critical thinking. Meaningful conversations can reveal a child's ability to analyze situations, draw connections, and think abstractly.

Documentation plays a crucial role in tracking progress over time. Keeping records of observations, conversations, and specific instances where critical thinking skills were displayed helps create a comprehensive picture of a child's development. These records serve as valuable references for setting goals and adapting teaching strategies.

Collaboration with educators and professionals can provide additional perspectives on a child's critical thinking progress. Sharing observations and insights with experts in early childhood development can offer fresh insights and recommendations for effectively supporting a child's cognitive growth.

Incorporating play-based assessments into the evaluation process can make tracking critical thinking skills more engaging for children. Games, puzzles, and interactive activities designed to assess problem-solving abilities provide valuable data and make the assessment process enjoyable for young learners.

Utilizing standardized tests to measure critical thinking skills can offer concrete metrics for evaluating progress. While not the sole indicator of a child's abilities, these tests can complement other evaluation methods by providing quantifiable data on areas such as analysis, inference, and evaluation skills.

By combining these diverse evaluation methods, caregivers can comprehensively understand a child's critical thinking abilities and effectively chart their progress over time. Each approach offers unique insights that contribute to a holistic view of the child's cognitive development, empowering caregivers to tailor their support and guidance to meet the specific needs of each young learner.

Evaluation Framework: Critical Thinking Development Model

In this framework for measuring critical thinking development in children, various components work together to provide a comprehensive approach to assessing and monitoring progress over time. Each part plays a crucial role in understanding and fostering critical thinking skills in young learners.

Definition of Critical Thinking Milestones

The framework begins by clearly defining appropriate critical thinking milestones for preschool-aged children. These milestones outline the expected behaviors and skills demonstrating essential thought, such as questioning, problem-solving, and connecting ideas. By defining these milestones, caregivers can have a clear roadmap of what to expect and work towards with their child.

Observing Behaviors and Skills

Identifying specific behaviors and skills that showcase critical thinking is vital. Observation methods should encompass structured activities, play, and daily routines to comprehensively capture a child's critical thinking abilities. Tools and techniques for recording these observations allow a detailed analysis of a child's progress over time.

Informal Assessments

Utilizing informal assessments like discussions and storytelling offers insights into a child's thought processes and understanding. These assessments provide a holistic view of how a child applies critical thinking skills in various contexts beyond structured tasks or puzzles.

Quantitative Measures

Including age-appropriate tasks or puzzles designed to evaluate critical thinking skills quantitatively is essential. Criteria for assessing performance on these tasks help quantify progress objectively. This quantitative aspect complements qualitative observations to paint a complete picture of a child's critical thinking abilities.

Self-Assessment and Reflection

Encouraging children to engage in self-assessment fosters metacognition and reflection on their learning journey. By involving children in reflecting on their problem-solving experiences, caregivers empower them to take an active role in their cognitive development.

Constructive Feedback

Providing constructive feedback is vital in nurturing a growth mindset in children. Positive reinforcement and guidance on areas for improvement create an environment where children feel motivated to enhance their critical thinking skills continuously.

Setting Realistic Goals

Setting individualized goals tailored to each child's developmental stage is crucial. These goals should be achievable yet challenging, promoting growth while acknowledging each child's unique pace of progress. Periodic reviews allow for adjustments based on evolving skills and interests.

This Evaluation Framework offers a structured approach to tracking critical thinking development in children, emphasizing the importance of qualitative and quantitative measures alongside self-assessment and constructive feedback mechanisms. By setting realistic goals based on defined milestones, caregivers can celebrate achievements along the way and support children effectively on their journey towards enhanced critical thinking skills.

Assess, Adapt, Achieve

Understanding the significance of assessing and monitoring a child's critical thinking development is fundamental. It's not just about recognizing where they stand but also about charting a path forward that recognizes their unique strengths and areas for growth. By implementing various evaluation methods, caregivers and educators can adapt their strategies effectively, ensuring that each child's educational journey is as rewarding as instructive.

Celebrate Every Step

Setting realistic milestones is crucial in the nurturing process. Celebrate large and small achievements to motivate young learners and reinforce their love for exploration and learning. This positive reinforcement helps build their confidence and encourages them to engage with challenges more readily, knowing they have a supportive network cheering them on.

Foster Creativity and Resilience

Emphasizing critical thinking from an early age does more than prepare children for academic success; it instills in them a lifelong love of learning. This approach fosters creativity, adaptability, and resilience—indispensable qualities in today's ever-changing world. Integrating critical thinking practices into daily activities prepares our children to face future challenges with assurance and ingenuity.

Take Action

As caregivers, you have the power to shape these young minds. Use the strategies discussed to monitor progress effectively and adapt learning environments to meet the evolving needs of each child. Remember, your efforts today set the foundation for tomorrow's innovators and leaders.

Let us move forward confidently, knowing we provide our

children with the tools they need to succeed in school and life. Let's continue to nurture these critical thinkers who will undoubtedly lead the way to a brighter future.

Chapter 8: Beyond the Box: Cultivating Creative Problem-Solvers

"The questions don't do the damage. Only the answers can do that."

J. K. Rowling

Unleashing Creative Minds: A Blueprint for the Future

In early childhood education, assessing and tracking progress in critical thinking is not just beneficial—it's imperative. By evaluating these skills, educators, and caregivers can pinpoint growth while identifying areas needing further development. This approach ensures that each child's journey towards becoming a creative problem-solver is monitored and nurtured effectively.

Understanding the importance of creativity and innovation in problem-solving begins with recognizing that these skills are pivotal in today's ever-changing world. Activities designed to foster imagination are not merely about having fun; they are crucial building blocks for developing the analytical prowess necessary for future challenges. From simple puzzles to complex group activities, each play-based scenario is a stepping stone toward enhancing a child's problem-solving toolkit.

The role of flexible thinking in boosting analytical abilities cannot be overstated. When children learn to view problems from multiple angles, they engage in deeper analysis. This flexibility is essential, equipping them to navigate varied and unexpected life situations. Encouraging such adaptability involves a range of strategies, from open-ended questions that prompt children to think on their feet to activities that require them to switch rules or perspectives midway.

Creating an environment that values and rewards out-of-the-box thinking is equally critical. This does not mean praising correct answers or traditional successes but acknowledging innovative approaches and unusual solutions. Such an environment not only celebrates creativity but also instills confidence in young learners, encouraging them to take risks and experiment without fear of failure.

To implement these strategies effectively, caregivers must adopt both a structured and an intuitive approach. This includes setting clear goals for creative development while being responsive to each child's unique needs and responses. Practical tools such as progress charts or portfolios can help track developments over time, offering tangible evidence of a child's creative journey.

Furthermore, a collaboration between educators, parents, and children is essential in cultivating an atmosphere where creative problem-solving thrives. Regular discussions about a child's progress can foster a more cohesive understanding of their developmental needs, ensuring that every stakeholder is aligned in nurturing critical thinking.

Finally, fostering critical thinking from an early age sets the groundwork for lifelong learning and adaptation. By prioritizing creativity and flexible thinking now, we prepare children for school and life—equipping them with the mental tools necessary to tackle any challenge with confidence and ingenuity. Engage actively with these strategies, vital to unlocking vast potential in every young mind you guide.

In fostering children's critical thinking skills, providing them with activities encouraging creative problem-solving is crucial. These activities are the foundation for developing innovative thinking and approaching challenges with a fresh perspective. By engaging children in tasks that require them to think outside the box, caregivers can nurture their ability to explore different solutions and embrace creativity as a tool for problem-solving.

One effective strategy is to incorporate open-ended questions into daily interactions with children. Instead of providing straightforward answers, please encourage them to think critically by asking questions that prompt deeper reflection. For example, when faced with a problem, ask them, "What do you think would happen if...?" This approach stimulates their curiosity and helps them consider various possibilities before finding a solution.

Another valuable technique is to introduce hands-on activities that promote experimentation and exploration. Building blocks, puzzles, art projects, and science experiments all offer opportunities for children to engage in trial-and-error problem-solving. These activities enhance their spatial awareness and fine motor skills, encourage them to think creatively and adapt their strategies based on the outcomes.

Furthermore, storytelling can be a powerful tool for nurturing creativity in children. Please encourage them to create stories or narratives, allowing their imagination to soar. Children learn to think flexibly and construct coherent narratives by inventing characters, settings, and plotlines. This skill translates into effective problem-solving by connecting disparate elements into a cohesive whole.

Engaging in role-playing scenarios can also stimulate creative thinking in children. Role-play encourages children to step into different perspectives and envision unique solutions to challenges, whether pretending to be scientists conducting experiments or explorers discovering new lands. This immersive experience fosters empathy, adaptability, and innovative thinking.

Nurturing Flexible Thinking in Young Minds

Flexible thinking plays a crucial role in enhancing a child's analytical abilities. Caregivers can empower young minds to approach challenges creatively and resiliently by fostering adaptability and openness to new ideas. Encouraging children to explore multiple solutions to a problem cultivates their capacity to think critically and consider diverse perspectives. Promoting a growth mindset where mistakes are viewed as learning opportunities rather than failures fosters a positive attitude toward problem-solving.

Flexibility in thinking allows children to navigate uncertainties and complexities with confidence. Teaching them to embrace ambiguity and seek alternative approaches helps build their cognitive agility. Exposing children to diverse viewpoints and encouraging them to think beyond conventional boundaries broadens their problem-solving repertoire. Creating an environment that celebrates innovation nurtures a child's inclination toward exploring unconventional solutions.

Engaging children in activities that require them to think on their feet and adapt quickly enhances their mental dexterity. Encouraging experimentation and risk-taking instills a sense of adventure in problem-solving, promoting out-of-the-box thinking. Providing opportunities for collaborative problem-solving allows children to benefit from collective intelligence and different perspectives, enriching their analytical skills.

Emphasizing the importance of perseverance in the face of challenges reinforces a child's resilience and determination. Celebrating small victories along the way motivates children to continue honing their critical thinking skills. Modeling flexible thinking as caregivers sets a powerful example for children, demonstrating the value of adaptability in overcoming obstacles.

By nurturing flexible thinking in children, caregivers equip them with essential skills for navigating an ever-changing world. Embracing uncertainty, seeking innovative solutions, and adapting to new circumstances become second nature when flexible thinking is ingrained early on. Encouraging children to approach problems with an open mind lays the foundation for lifelong learning and growth, empowering them to tackle challenges confidently and creatively.

Creating an environment that values and rewards out-of-the-box thinking is crucial for nurturing young minds to become innovative problem-solvers. Encouraging creativity in children involves setting the stage for exploration, experimentation, and open-mindedness. Offering a safe space where unconventional ideas are welcomed can boost a child's confidence in expressing unique solutions to challenges. Praise and acknowledgment for creativity, even if the idea doesn't work out as planned, can reinforce the importance of thinking creatively rather than sticking to conventional methods.

Incorporating play into learning environments can significantly enhance a child's ability to think outside the box. Play allows children to engage in imaginative scenarios, explore different perspectives, and test new ideas without fear of failure. Providing open-ended materials such as blocks, art supplies, or puzzles encourages children to think creatively and develop innovative solutions independently.

Modeling creative thinking is another effective way to instill a value for out-of-the-box ideas in children. When caregivers demonstrate flexibility in problem-solving, children learn by example and are more likely to adopt similar strategies. Engaging in collaborative activities where brainstorming and sharing ideas are encouraged can also foster a culture of creativity among children.

Creating a supportive environment that values out-of-the-box thinking involves celebrating diversity in perspectives and approaches. By exposing children to different cultures, backgrounds, and ways of thinking, caregivers can broaden their understanding of what constitutes creative problem-solving. Encouraging curiosity and a sense of wonder about the world can ignite a child's imagination and drive to explore unconventional solutions to their problems.

Setting realistic expectations for creative thinking while providing constructive feedback helps children understand the value of persistence and resilience in problem-solving.

Caregivers can motivate children to continue exploring new ideas and approaches by acknowledging efforts rather than just outcomes. Establishing a growth mindset that embraces challenges as learning opportunities can cultivate a lifelong appreciation for creative problem-solving skills.

Cultivating Creative Problem-Solvers: A Necessity, Not an Option

In an increasingly complex and interconnected world, fostering creative problem-solving skills from an early age is not just beneficial—it's essential. We've explored activities that encourage creativity and enhance a child's analytical abilities through flexible thinking. More importantly, we've created environments that reward and value innovative thinking. These strategies are vital for developing minds ready to tackle the challenges and opportunities of tomorrow.

Tracking Progress is Key

The significance of assessing and monitoring a child's development in critical thinking cannot be overstated. Regular evaluation helps identify not just areas of strength but also areas needing improvement, enabling targeted interventions that foster better outcomes. It is crucial to understand that this tracking isn't just about measuring—it's about understanding each child's unique journey in cognitive development.

Implement Practical Solutions

Simple yet effective methods can be implemented to track and enhance critical thinking in young learners. For instance, maintaining a progress journal can help educators and parents see patterns over time, adjust strategies as needed, and provide consistent feedback that encourages children to grow. Tools such as checklists or structured reflections can also play a significant role in this ongoing assessment process.

Empower Through Action

As caregivers and educators, you can shape these young minds. Use the insights from assessments to tailor learning experiences that challenge and engage children. Remember, every child has the potential to think creatively; they only need the right environment and encouragement to unlock this ability.

Engage with Confidence

Take these strategies forward with confidence. By consistently applying these practices, you are providing children with a robust foundation in critical thinking. This skill will serve them well beyond their early years into all facets of life. Your proactive engagement can make a profound difference in their lifelong learning journey.

By nurturing these critical skills today, we prepare our children for a future where they solve problems and innovate solutions that we have yet to imagine. Let us commit to diligent efforts, ensuring our young learners are equipped to thrive in an ever-evolving world.

Chapter 9: Engaging Young Minds: The Key to Practice and Retention

"We cannot solve our problems with the same thinking we used when we created them."

Albert Einstein

Unleashing the Power of Play: Transforming Theory into Thrilling Learning Adventures

In an era of rapidly evolving education, the imperative to equip our youngest with adept critical thinking skills has never been more pressing. The landscape of early childhood development is rich with opportunities to nurture a curious and analytical mindset, mainly through creative problem-solving activities. Engaging young minds through innovative and interactive methods enriches their cognitive abilities and sets a robust foundation for lifelong learning and adaptability.

Identifying engaging interactive resources is fundamental in making critical thinking exercises appealing to children. In this digital age, educational apps, websites, and games play a pivotal role in engagingly delivering these skills. Each resource should be carefully selected to match the child's developmental stage and cognitive abilities, ensuring that the challenges presented are neither manageable nor daunting. For instance, apps that simulate puzzle-solving scenarios can enhance spatial reasoning and logical thinking.

Moreover, integrating theoretical concepts with practical applications significantly boosts retention and understanding. When children apply what they've learned in theory through tangible activities, the learning experience becomes more concrete and memorable. For example, simple household items demonstrating basic physics concepts can turn an abstract lesson into an interactive science experiment, fostering curiosity and excitement about learning.

The choice of learning tools should be diverse to accommodate various teaching styles and preferences. From tactile resources like blocks and puzzles that encourage manual manipulation to storybooks that expand imagination and problem-solving capabilities, each tool serves a unique purpose in developing critical thinking. This diversity keeps children engaged and helps them discover their preferred learning modalities.

Crafting Customized Cognitive Challenges

Personalizing the learning experience plays a crucial role in maintaining engagement. Educators can maximize enjoyment and educational value by tailoring activities to align with individual interests and developmental levels. This customization might involve adjusting the difficulty level of puzzles or choosing story themes that resonate with the child's interests.

Engagement strategies must also include reflective practices for educators and parents. Regularly assessing the effectiveness of the tools and methods used allows for continual adaptation and improvement, ensuring that the learning experiences remain practical and relevant. Reflection can involve observing children's responses to different activities, soliciting feedback from them directly, or discussing outcomes with fellow educators.

A Blueprint for Building Better Thinkers

Step by Step: "Cognitive Constructors"

The objective is To equip children with robust critical thinking skills through engaging, practical experiences that bridge theory with reality.

1. **Interactive Resources for Critical Thinking Exercises**
    - List educational apps like "Thinkrolls," which teach logic through fun physics puzzles.
    - Discuss age appropriateness, ensuring the complexity matches the child's cognitive stage.
    - Timeframe: Continuously update and review resources every few months to keep up with developmental changes.

2. **Pairing Theoretical Concepts with Practical Activities**
    - Use everyday items for experiments; for example, demonstrate gravity using a ball.
    - Step-by-step guide on setting up simple yet

effective science experiments at home.

- Timeframe: Integrate these activities weekly to reinforce theoretical knowledge practically.

3. **Choosing a Variety of Learning Tools**

- Include manipulatives such as building blocks for younger children to improve spatial awareness.

- Adapt tools based on feedback from usage; some may prefer visual aids over tactile ones.

- Timeframe: Assess tool effectiveness quarterly; introduce new tools bi-annually.

4. **Personalizing Learning Experiences**

    - Tailor activities based on observed preferences—modify difficulty or introduce new concepts accordingly.

    - Monitor progress and adjust approaches; what works today might not work as well tomorrow.

    - Timeframe: Personalize learning sessions monthly based on ongoing assessments.

5. **Reflecting on Engagement Strategies**

    - Implement reflective sessions post-activity to gauge what was most or least effective.

- o Encourage open dialogue about preferences and difficulties faced during learning.
- o Timeframe: Reflect after each significant activity; refine strategies continually over time.

By systematically applying these steps, educators can foster an environment where young learners enthusiastically tackle challenges and develop a deep-seated love for discovery and innovation—cornerstones of lifelong critical thinking.

Children's engagement in critical thinking exercises can be significantly enhanced using interactive resources that appeal to their curiosity and creativity. When selecting tools for young minds, it is essential to consider their age, interests, and developmental stage. Interactive games, puzzles, and storytelling platforms can captivate children's attention while challenging them to think critically. These resources provide an enjoyable way for children to practice problem-solving skills dynamically and engagingly. By incorporating these interactive elements into learning activities, educators can foster a positive attitude towards critical thinking in children from an early age.

Encouraging Participation:

Encouraging active participation rather than passive observation is crucial to make critical thinking exercises appealing to children. Interactive resources that require hands-on engagement prompt children to think, analyze, and solve problems actively. Activities that involve physical movement, collaboration with peers, or creative expression can stimulate children's cognitive abilities while keeping them interested and motivated. Educators can instill a love for critical thinking in young learners by creating a supportive environment encouraging experimentation and exploration.

Variety in Learning Tools:

Introducing a variety of interactive resources can cater to different learning styles and preferences among children. Some may excel in visual tasks, while others prefer auditory or kinesthetic activities. By diversifying the tools used for critical thinking exercises, educators can accommodate the diverse needs of their students and create a more inclusive learning experience. Tools such as interactive whiteboards, educational apps, manipulatives, and role-playing games offer multiple avenues for children to engage with complex concepts and develop problem-solving skills.

Real-World Relevance:

Connecting critical thinking exercises to real-world scenarios can enhance children's understanding and motivation to participate actively. By incorporating practical examples or challenges that relate to everyday life experiences, educators can demonstrate the relevance of critical thinking skills in solving problems and making informed decisions. Engaging children in discussions about how critical thinking applies beyond the classroom setting fosters a deeper appreciation for these skills and encourages them to use their knowledge in various contexts.

Engagement through Creativity:

Creativity plays a significant role in making critical thinking exercises appealing to children. Encouraging imaginative thinking, brainstorming sessions, or open-ended questions allows children to creatively explore multiple solutions to a problem. Incorporating art projects, storytelling activities, or design challenges into critical thinking exercises stimulates children's creativity while honing their analytical skills. Educators empower children to approach challenges with innovation and resilience by fostering a creative mindset alongside essential thinking abilities.

Enhancing Learning Retention through Practical Activities

Pairing theoretical concepts with engaging practical activities is essential for enhancing learning retention in young minds. Children can grasp complex concepts more effectively by bridging the gap between abstract ideas and hands-on experiences. One powerful method is introducing interactive games requiring critical thinking skills while reinforcing theoretical knowledge. For example, combining a lesson on shapes with a puzzle game can help children apply their learning fun and engagingly. This approach solidifies their understanding and cultivates a deeper connection to the subject matter.

Another effective strategy is to create real-world scenarios that mirror theoretical principles. For instance, when teaching about measurements, setting up a cooking activity where children need to follow a recipe can reinforce the concept of units and quantities. Educators can significantly boost retention rates by immersing children in practical tasks related to the theory they are learning. The key lies in making the activities relatable and enjoyable, turning abstract ideas into tangible experiences that leave a lasting impression on young minds.

Incorporating multisensory elements into learning experiences can also enhance retention by engaging different modalities of perception. Utilizing visual aids, hands-on materials, and auditory cues can cater to various learning styles, ensuring that every child has the opportunity to absorb and retain information effectively. By appealing to multiple senses, educators create a dynamic learning environment that caters to diverse learners' needs and maximizes knowledge retention.

Practical activities should be designed with clear learning objectives, aligning them closely with the theoretical concepts taught. This alignment ensures that every activity serves a specific educational purpose, reinforcing key ideas and promoting more profound understanding. Educators can create a cohesive learning experience that encourages retention through meaningful engagement by structuring activities around core learning outcomes.

Encouraging experimentation and exploration in practical activities allows children to apply theoretical concepts creatively. By fostering an environment where trial and error are embraced, educators empower children to think critically and problem-solve independently. This approach reinforces theoretical knowledge and instills confidence in young learners as they navigate challenges and discover solutions through hands-on experience.

When engaging young minds, choosing diverse learning tools that cater to various educator and learner preferences is essential. Each child is unique, and what works well for one may not necessarily work for another. Flexibility in your approach is critical to ensuring optimal engagement and learning retention. By offering a variety of tools, you create a dynamic learning environment that can accommodate different learning styles and preferences.

Visual learners may benefit significantly from educational videos, infographics, or colorful diagrams that help them grasp concepts more quickly. Auditory learners, on the other hand, might excel with podcasts, music, or verbal instructions that allow them to absorb information through listening. Kinesthetic learners, who learn best through hands-on activities, could thrive with interactive games, experiments, or role-playing exercises that involve movement and tactile experiences.

Technology can also be a powerful ally in engaging young minds. Educational apps, interactive websites, and online platforms designed specifically for children can make learning more exciting and accessible. Incorporating digital tools not only adds an element of fun but also introduces children to essential skills they will need in the digital age.

Furthermore, collaborative activities can foster social interaction and teamwork skills while enhancing the learning experience. Group projects, peer-to-peer discussions, and cooperative games can encourage children to share ideas, communicate effectively, and learn from one another. Collaboration enriches the educational journey and prepares children for real-world situations where teamwork is often required.

In addition to traditional tools like textbooks and workbooks, consider incorporating hands-on materials such as building blocks, puzzles, art supplies, or science kits. These tangible resources stimulate young learners' creativity, critical thinking, and problem-solving abilities. By providing multisensory experiences, you cater to different learning modalities and deepen children's understanding of various concepts.

Remember that the goal is to create a stimulating learning environment that nurtures curiosity and encourages exploration. By offering diverse learning tools that align with different preferences and styles, you empower children to engage actively with the material and retain knowledge more effectively. Variety is critical in capturing young minds' attention and fostering a lifelong love for learning.

As we reflect on the strategies discussed, it is clear that engaging young minds effectively is pivotal for nurturing their problem-solving skills. By carefully selecting interactive resources that captivate and challenge, educators can foster an environment where critical thinking becomes both a habit and a joy for children. This supports cognitive growth and prepares them for future complexities in an ever-evolving world.

Practical activities, when paired with theoretical concepts, significantly enhance learning retention. This hands-on approach ensures that children can see the relevance of their learning in everyday situations, making the abstract concepts of critical thinking tangible and accessible. Educators need to weave these activities into the fabric of learning to maintain a dynamic and stimulating educational experience.

Moreover, understanding and accommodating different preferences in learning tools is crucial. Every educator and learner brings unique strengths and needs to the table. By diversifying our tools—digital apps, physical puzzles, or interactive group tasks—we cater to these varied styles, enhancing engagement across all types of young thinkers.

Take action by integrating these tools and strategies into your teaching or parenting methods. Observe how they improve engagement and foster a deeper understanding and application of critical thinking skills in children's everyday lives.

Remember, each step you take towards enriching your educational approach reverberates through every aspect of a child's development. Empowering them with the skills to think critically and solve problems creatively opens doors to endless possibilities in their futures. Equip them today for the challenges of tomorrow with confidence and competence.

Chapter 10: Reading for Reasoning: Building a Foundation with Books

"Critical thinking is, in short, self-directed, self-disciplined, self-monitored, and self-corrective thinking."

Paul and Elder

Unlocking the Mind: How Books Shape Our Youngest Thinkers

Developing critical thinking skills begins not in the classroom or the boardroom but in the cozy corners of nurseries and playrooms where young children first encounter books. Early exposure to reading is not just about learning language—it is a foundational step in shaping analytical minds capable of reasoning and questioning. This chapter delves into how carefully selected books can stimulate cognitive growth and make learning an interactive, engaging experience for children.

Research consistently shows that children who engage with cognitive development books from an early age exhibit enhanced abilities to analyze, reason, and solve problems. These aren't merely academic skills but essential life skills that help children navigate the complex world around them. By introducing young readers to books that challenge their understanding and expand their curiosity, parents and educators can lay a robust foundation for lifelong learning and critical thinking.

Selecting suitable materials, however, is crucial. It's not just about picking up any book off the shelf. Parents and educators need to choose reading materials that are age-appropriate yet challenging, balancing complexity with what is comprehensible for young minds. This balance ensures that children are neither bored by what is too easy nor overwhelmed by what is too complex.

Furthermore, incorporating these books into daily routines is vital. Regular reading sessions are more than literacy exercises; they allow children to ask questions, explore concepts, and connect ideas. Each session should be a stepping stone towards building a habit of inquiry and reflection.

To make these sessions effective, interactive tools such as worksheets, flashcards, and lesson plans tailored to the content of the books can be incredibly beneficial. These tools transform reading from a passive activity into an active exploration, prompting children to engage with the material on multiple levels. They also provide practical ways for children to apply what they have learned, reinforcing their understanding and retention of complex ideas.

Parents and educators play a pivotal role here. They can encourage deeper thinking by asking probing questions and guiding discussions about the stories and concepts in books. For instance, after reading a story, a parent might ask, "What would you have done if you were in that situation?" or "Why do you think this character acted this way?" Such questions stimulate critical thinking and help children understand various perspectives.

Lastly, it's essential to create an environment that celebrates curiosity. A home or classroom where questions are welcomed and explored nurtures young minds eager to learn and unafraid to challenge ideas. This environment supports cognitive development and encourages children to become confident learners who view education as a dynamic and interactive process.

We can ensure our children develop strong reasoning skills from a very young age by strategically selecting books, integrating engaging tools, and nurturing an environment rich in dialogue and inquiry. These efforts will equip them with the critical thinking abilities necessary for success in school and beyond.

Early exposure to cognitive development books is pivotal in shaping a child's analytical thinking skills. The impact of introducing children to thought-provoking literature from a young age cannot be overstated. By engaging with books that stimulate curiosity, encourage questioning, and promote critical thinking, children develop the foundation necessary for advanced cognitive abilities later in life. These early interactions with books lay the groundwork for reasoning, problem-solving, and decision-making skills essential for navigating the world's complexities.

Reading as a Tool for Cognitive Development

Books are not merely sources of information but powerful tools for cognitive development. When children are exposed to diverse reading materials that challenge their minds, they think critically, analyze situations, and draw connections between different concepts. Reading introduces them to new ideas, perspectives, and ways of thinking, expanding their cognitive abilities and fostering creativity.

Nurturing Analytical Thinking

Early exposure to cognitive development books nurtures analytical thinking by encouraging children to explore, question, and evaluate information. Children learn to approach challenges with a critical mindset through stories that prompt reflection, puzzles that require problem-solving skills, and activities that engage their logical reasoning. This early cultivation of analytical thinking sets the stage for a lifetime of learning and growth.

Building a Foundation for Reasoning

Books provide a solid foundation for reasoning skills by presenting children with scenarios that require them to make connections, draw conclusions, and form logical arguments. Children learn to assess evidence, weigh options, and arrive at informed decisions as they engage with characters facing dilemmas or puzzles that demand solutions. This reasoning process is essential for developing sound judgment and practical problem-solving abilities.

Embracing the Journey Towards Critical Thinking

By recognizing the profound impact of early exposure to cognitive development books on fostering analytical thinking, parents and educators can actively incorporate such materials into a child's learning environment. Through interactive reading sessions, thought-provoking discussions, and engaging activities inspired by these books, children can embark on a journey towards honing their critical thinking skills. This intentional approach to nurturing analytical thinking sets the stage for young minds' continued growth and intellectual development.

When selecting reading materials to challenge and expand a child's cognitive abilities, consider the depth and complexity of the content, opt for books that introduce new concepts, provoke thought, and encourage critical thinking. Look for stories with diverse characters and settings to broaden a child's perspective and promote empathy. Choose books incorporating problem-solving scenarios or moral dilemmas to stimulate analytical thinking.

Engage children with interactive reading experiences by selecting books that invite participation. Look for titles that include questions for discussion, activities related to the story, or prompts for creative thinking. Encourage children to predict the plot or characters, fostering their ability to think ahead and anticipate outcomes.

Select books that align with your child's interests, whether they are fascinated by animals, space, history, or fantasy. Tailoring reading materials to a child's preferences increases engagement and motivation to explore new ideas. Rotate genres and themes to expose children to various concepts and writing styles, keeping their interest piqued.

Incorporate multisensory elements into reading sessions by choosing books with tactile components, sound effects, or interactive features. These enhancements can deepen a child's understanding of the story and encourage active participation in the reading experience. Utilize props or visual aids to bring the narrative to life and stimulate different senses.

Encourage critical thinking by selecting books that prompt reflection and analysis. Choose stories that raise thought-provoking questions or present complex moral dilemmas for discussion. Encourage children to express their opinions on the characters' choices or the outcomes of the plot, fostering independent thought and reasoning skills.

When introducing challenging reading materials, provide support and guidance as needed. Encourage children to ask questions, seek clarification, and share their thoughts on the content. Create a safe space for open dialogue about complex topics or confusing concepts, nurturing a child's confidence in their ability to tackle complex ideas.

By carefully selecting reading materials that challenge and expand a child's cognitive abilities, you can foster a love for learning and cultivate critical thinking skills early on. Remember that each child is unique, so be flexible and adapt reading selections to suit their interests and learning styles. Embrace the journey of exploration and discovery through books that inspire curiosity, spark imagination, and lay the foundation for a lifetime of analytical thinking.

Incorporating age-appropriate cognitive development literature into daily learning sessions can be a powerful tool to spark curiosity and foster critical thinking in young minds. Parents and educators can inspire a love for learning and exploration by introducing engaging books that challenge children's cognitive abilities. Reading sessions should focus on storytelling, prompting questions, and encouraging discovery. Selecting books that align with the child's developmental stage ensures the content is stimulating and comprehensible.

When choosing reading materials, consider the child's interests, preferences, and current level of cognitive development. Opt for books that introduce new concepts, vocabulary, and ideas to expand their understanding of the world around them. Interactive books with flaps, textures, or puzzles can enhance engagement and encourage active participation during reading sessions. Additionally, seek books that prompt critical thinking by posing thought-provoking questions or presenting moral dilemmas for discussion.

To make the most of cognitive development literature, it is essential to integrate these reading sessions seamlessly into daily routines. Designate a specific time each day for reading, creating a cozy and inviting environment free from distractions. Encourage children to ask questions, make predictions, and connect the story to their experiences. This interactive approach not only enhances comprehension but also nurtures analytical thinking skills.

Engaging in discussions after reading sessions can further deepen the child's understanding and critical thinking abilities. Please encourage them to express their thoughts, share opinions, and debate different viewpoints in the book. Ask open-ended questions that promote reflection and analysis, fostering a habit of questioning and reasoning in young learners.

Incorporating age-appropriate cognitive development literature into daily routines can transform reading sessions into valuable learning opportunities. Parents and educators can inspire a thirst for knowledge and nurture critical thinking skills early by selecting stimulating books that challenge children's cognitive abilities. Encouraging active participation, fostering discussions, and connecting stories to real-life situations can enrich the reading experience and lay a solid foundation for analytical thinking in young minds.

Books are more than just stories; they are tools that shape young minds into analytical thinkers capable of tackling complex challenges. Recognizing the impact of cognitive development books is the first step toward nurturing a child's ability to reason and inquire. Selecting materials that challenge and expand their cognitive skills empowers them to think deeper and broader.

Incorporating age-appropriate literature into daily learning sessions transforms routine reading into an adventure of questions and discovery. This practice engages children and stimulates their curiosity and critical thinking skills. Choosing books that entertain and provoke thought is essential, encouraging children to explore ideas beyond the text.

Interactive resources, such as worksheets and flashcards, complement these reading sessions, making learning dynamic and retention more robust. The synergy between theoretical concepts and practical activities enriches the learning experience, ensuring children grasp and apply their knowledge effectively.

Take control of your educational approach by integrating these strategies into daily interactions with children. Your role in facilitating their cognitive development is crucial. Remember, each book read is a step towards building a stronger foundation for complex thought processes in your child's future.

By fostering an environment rich in challenges and discoveries through carefully selected books and interactive tools, you set the stage for significant cognitive growth. Engage actively with these strategies, witness the transformative power of reading, and watch young minds flourish into critical thinkers ready to conquer the world's wonders.

Chapter 11: Learning Reimagined: Innovative Approaches to Thinking

"The unexamined life is not worth living."

Socrates

Are You Ready to Transform How Your Child Thinks?

In an era where critical thinking is more important than ever, early childhood represents a golden opportunity to lay a strong foundation. Cognitive development is not just about learning facts; it's about shaping how a child processes information, solves problems, and understands complex concepts. This chapter delves into the transformative power of innovative teaching methods designed specifically for young learners. These methods capture their interest and significantly boost their critical thinking abilities from a tender age.

Early exposure to structured cognitive development activities can profoundly impact a child's critical thinking ability. Introducing children to age-appropriate materials that challenge their understanding opens up new pathways in their brains. These pathways are crucial for developing analytical skills to serve them throughout their lives. Books and activities tailored for cognitive enhancement are more than just educational tools; they are gateways to intellectual growth and curiosity.

The role of novelty in maintaining children's engagement cannot be overstated. Young minds are inherently curious and eager to explore new things. By continuously introducing novel learning experiences, we keep their enthusiasm for learning alive. This makes the learning process enjoyable and effective, as engagement is critical to deeper understanding and retention of knowledge.

Implementing unique and progressive learning experiences is essential for fostering an environment where exploration and curiosity are encouraged. These experiences should not be mundane or repetitive but challenge the child's intellect and provoke questions. Such an environment promotes active learning, where children are not just passive recipients of information but actively seek knowledge and solutions.

Parents and educators often wonder how best to implement

these strategies effectively. The answer lies in being proactive and intentional about the educational content and activities presented to children. It involves selecting materials that align with developmental stages and pushing the boundaries of what children can understand at their age.

Caregivers must be equipped with practical tools and clear guidance to successfully implement these strategies. This includes understanding which types of books and activities best suit different age groups and how to present them engagingly. Additionally, caregivers must remain curious learners who continue seeking new methods and innovations in early childhood education.

By embracing these innovative approaches to thinking, caregivers can dramatically enhance the cognitive development of young learners. This prepares them for academic success and instills a lifelong love for learning and critical inquiry. Remember, every child has the potential to think critically; it's our job to unlock this potential through thoughtful, engaging, and innovative educational practices.

Innovative teaching methods are crucial in capturing children's interest and fostering critical thinking skills from an early age. Traditional educational approaches may not always be sufficient to stimulate young minds effectively. By exploring alternative methods that align with children's natural curiosity and eagerness to learn, caregivers can unlock new pathways for cognitive development.

Engagement is Key: Keeping children engaged is essential for effective learning. Introducing interactive activities, hands-on experiments, and creative projects can spark curiosity and encourage critical thinking. These engaging experiences make learning fun and help children retain information better and apply it in different contexts.

Personalized Learning: Every child has unique learning styles and preferences. Tailoring teaching methods to suit a child's specific needs can enhance their understanding and retention of information. By recognizing each child's strengths and weaknesses, caregivers can effectively provide personalized learning experiences that cater to their cognitive development.

Multisensory Approaches: Utilizing a variety of sensory experiences in teaching can deepen a child's understanding of complex concepts. Incorporating visual aids, hands-on activities, music, and movement into lessons can create a holistic learning environment that appeals to different learning styles. This multisensory approach enhances engagement and promotes critical thinking by stimulating multiple senses simultaneously.

Encouraging Exploration: Encouraging children to explore diverse topics and ideas can broaden their perspective and enhance their critical thinking abilities. Providing opportunities for independent research, field trips, or guest speakers can expose children to new information and inspire them to think critically about the world.

Collaborative Learning: Collaborative activities promote teamwork, communication skills, and critical thinking as children work together to solve problems or complete tasks. Group projects, discussions, and peer-to-peer learning encourage children to consider different viewpoints, think creatively, and analyze information collectively.

Technology Integration: Integrating technology into learning experiences can enhance engagement and provide interactive tools for critical thinking development. Educational apps, online resources, and digital platforms offer innovative ways to present information, encourage problem-solving, and foster analytical skills in children.

Recognize the Importance of Novelty in Maintaining Children's Engagement in Learning Activities

In early childhood education, novelty is crucial in sustaining children's interest and engagement in learning activities. Children thrive on new experiences and challenges, which stimulate their curiosity and foster a sense of exploration. By introducing novel elements into their learning environment, caregivers can capture children's attention and ignite their passion for discovering the world around them.

Embracing Novelty as a Catalyst for Engagement

Novelty sparks excitement and keeps children motivated to learn. Introducing fresh perspectives, diverse materials, and unique approaches to teaching can invigorate children's cognitive processes. By incorporating novel elements into lessons and activities, caregivers can create a dynamic learning environment that encourages active participation and critical thinking. Novelty cultivates a sense of wonder and curiosity, inspiring children to delve deeper into complex concepts and develop analytical skills.

The Power of Surprise and Innovation

Surprise in learning activities can trigger a child's wonder and delight. Introducing unexpected twists or innovative methods can captivate children's attention and encourage them to explore new ideas enthusiastically. Incorporating surprises into educational experiences can enhance memory retention, boost creativity, and promote problem-solving skills. By embracing surprise as a tool for engagement, caregivers can create memorable learning moments that impact children's cognitive development.

Balancing Familiarity With Novelty

While novelty is essential for maintaining children's engagement, it is also crucial to strike a balance with familiar elements. Combining the comfort of familiarity with the excitement of novelty creates a harmonious learning environment that supports both exploration and security. Caregivers can introduce new concepts gradually, building upon existing knowledge to expand children's understanding while ensuring they feel confident and supported in their learning journey.

Practical Strategies for Integrating Novelty

- **Introduce new materials:** Bring age-appropriate books, toys, or tools that expose children to unfamiliar concepts.

- **Experiment with different teaching methods:** Incorporate hands-on activities, group projects, or multimedia resources to diversify the learning experience.

- **Encourage exploration:** Create open-ended play and discovery opportunities to stimulate children's natural curiosity.

- **Rotate learning environments:** Switch up the physical setting or layout of the learning space to provide fresh perspectives and stimulate creativity.

- **Celebrate achievements:** Acknowledge and reward

children's efforts in exploring new ideas or overcoming challenges to reinforce positive associations with novelty.

By recognizing the significance of novelty in maintaining children's engagement in learning activities, caregivers can create dynamic educational experiences that inspire curiosity, promote critical thinking, and nurture a lifelong love for learning.

Framework: Innovative Teaching Model for Critical Thinking Development

The innovative teaching model presented here aims to foster critical thinking skills in children through unique and progressive learning experiences. This model provides a structured approach to creating engaging activities stimulating young learners' curiosity, exploration, and analytical thinking.

Identifying Interests and Curiosities

The first step of the model involves identifying interests and curiosities specific to the age group of children. Educators and caregivers can tailor learning experiences to resonate with their natural inclinations by understanding what captivates their attention. This customization ensures that activities are engaging and relevant to the children's developmental stage, maximizing the impact on their critical thinking abilities.

Thematic Learning Integration

Thematic learning is a core element of this model, emphasizing exploring a single theme across various disciplines such as science, literature, and art. By integrating thematic learning, children are encouraged to make connections between different subjects and see the broader application of concepts. This multidisciplinary approach enriches their understanding and nurtures their ability to think critically about complex topics.

Creating Immersive Learning Environments

Central to the model is creating immersive learning environments that simulate real-world scenarios. These environments provide children with hands-on experiences where they can apply critical thinking skills to solve problems or complete projects. For example, setting up a 'marketplace' allows children to learn about math, social skills, and basic economics through interactive play, fostering a holistic understanding of concepts.

Incorporating Technology and Balancing Screen Time

In today's digital age, it is crucial to incorporate technology into learning experiences while maintaining a balance with hands-on activities. The model suggests using age-appropriate digital tools like coding apps or interactive storybooks to promote critical thinking skills. By leveraging technology effectively, educators can enhance children's analytical abilities while ensuring they engage in diverse learning modalities beyond screens.

Encouraging Reflection and Discussion

After completing activities, it is essential to encourage reflection and discussion among children. This post-activity phase guides educators and parents on how to ask open-ended questions that prompt children to explain their thinking processes and conclusions. By fostering metacognition through reflection, children learn to articulate their thoughts clearly, enhancing their ability to think critically about various scenarios.

Practical Implications

This innovative teaching model offers practical implications for educators and caregivers seeking to enhance children's critical thinking skills. Following this systematic approach, they can create dynamic learning experiences that captivate children's interest and promote analytical thinking. The model's emphasis on customization, thematic integration, immersive environments, technology usage, and reflection ensures a comprehensive strategy for nurturing critical thinking from an early age.

In summary, this innovative teaching model provides a roadmap for implementing unique learning experiences that encourage exploration and curiosity while fostering critical thinking in children. Following the framework outlined here, educators and caregivers can create enriching environments where young learners can thrive intellectually and develop essential cognitive skills for navigating an ever-changing world.

We have unveiled effective strategies to foster critical thinking in young children by exploring innovative teaching methods, recognizing the importance of novelty, and implementing unique learning experiences. Engaging them early with cognitive development books captures their interest and expands their understanding of complex concepts. This approach ensures that the foundational skills necessary for analytical thinking are built robustly and resiliently.

It is essential to remember that each child's learning journey is unique. By tailoring educational activities to their inherent curiosity and desire for exploration, caregivers can significantly enhance a child's engagement and retention of knowledge. Simple, practical strategies such as introducing age-appropriate cognitive development materials can substantially affect their mental growth.

Empower yourself as a caregiver by utilizing these tools to create a fun and fruitful learning environment. You can shape these young minds into critical thinkers who will question the world around them and possess the skills to find answers.

Encourage consistent engagement with these innovative methods. The more actively you incorporate these approaches into daily learning activities, the more profound the impact on your child's development will be. This is not merely about education; it's about setting a foundation for lifelong learning and curiosity.

Remember, your role is crucial in this transformative process. By embracing these strategies, you are not just educating but inspiring. You are building a future where critical thinking is second nature, ensuring your child is well-equipped to face the world's wonders with confidence and curiosity. Let us step forward with the assurance that our efforts today will cultivate the thinkers of tomorrow.

Chapter 12: The Game Changer: Stimulating Minds with Play

"Thinking should become your capital asset, no matter whatever ups and downs you come across in your life."

A.P.J. Abdul Kalam

Igniting Young Minds: The Transformative Power of Play in Learning

The education journey continuously evolves, adapting to discoveries about how young minds learn best. Traditional methods heavily relying on rote learning are challenged by innovative approaches that engage and stimulate children's critical thinking. This chapter delves into how brain games and puzzles are pivotal tools in enhancing a child's cognitive abilities and shaping problem-solving skills from an early age.

Research underscores the profound impact that play can have on developing reasoning skills. By integrating brain games into daily learning routines, children are exposed to scenarios that require them to think critically and adapt swiftly. These games often present problems in a playful context, making learning enjoyable and impactful. Caregivers and educators need to understand that such activities do more than entertain; they build the foundations of analytical thinking.

Expanding on this notion, exploring various cognitive games across different settings is crucial. These games can be seamlessly woven into multiple parts of a child's day, whether at home, in classrooms, or outdoors. The versatility of puzzle-based activities or strategy games enhances their appeal and allows for repeated practice, which is crucial in mastering problem-solving skills. The integration of these games should be strategic, aiming to challenge the child progressively as their skills develop.

Creating a balanced routine is equally important. While brain-stimulating activities are valuable, they must be part of a broader educational plan that includes physical play, creative arts, and downtime. This balanced approach ensures comprehensive cognitive development, catering to a child's growth. It helps prevent any one area from becoming overwhelming or neglected.

Moreover, the role of caregivers and educators is to provide these tools and actively participate in these interactive play sessions. Adults' engagement enhances learning outcomes and strengthens emotional bonds, providing a secure environment for children to explore new challenges.

The benefits of implementing playful learning strategies extend beyond immediate educational outcomes; they help instill a lifelong love for learning and curiosity. Children taught through interactive and engaging methods are more likely to develop into adults who approach problems with an open mind and resilience.

To effectively apply these strategies, caregivers must be equipped with practical approaches that are easy to implement. This includes choosing age-appropriate games that align with the child's cognitive abilities and interests. Furthermore, it involves observing the child's responses to different types of games and adjusting the complexity or variety accordingly.

This chapter will give readers valuable insights into transforming traditional learning environments into dynamic spaces where young minds thrive. Emphasizing action over passive reception accelerates cognitive development and builds confident learners ready to easily navigate the world's complexities.

Understanding how brain games and puzzles amplify critical thinking and reasoning skills is essential for caregivers looking to enhance their children's cognitive development. These activities are not just entertaining pastimes but powerful tools to stimulate young minds and foster essential problem-solving and logical reasoning skills. By engaging children in brain games and puzzles, caregivers can provide them with opportunities to practice critical thinking in a fun and interactive way.

Brain games and puzzles come in various forms, from traditional jigsaw puzzles to modern digital games designed to challenge cognitive abilities. These activities require children to use analytical skills, memory, and creativity to solve problems. As children navigate through the complexities of these challenges, they learn to think critically, consider different perspectives, and explore innovative solutions. This process helps them develop resilience, adaptability, and a growth mindset.

Moreover, brain games and puzzles promote concentration and focus. When engrossed in solving a puzzle or unraveling a complex problem, children learn to pay attention to details, think methodically, and stay engaged for extended periods. This heightened focus translates into improved academic performance and better retention of information.

Another benefit of brain games and puzzles is their ability to boost confidence. As children successfully tackle challenging tasks and overcome obstacles in these activities, they build self-assurance in their problem-solving skills. This newfound confidence spills over into other areas of their lives, empowering them to face challenges positively.

Nurturing Critical Thinking Through Cognitive Games

By incorporating brain games and puzzles into a child's daily routine, caregivers can create an enriching learning environment that nurtures critical thinking skills from an early age.

Integrating various cognitive games into teaching strategies is a powerful tool to enhance problem-solving capabilities in young children. By incorporating games that challenge their thinking and reasoning skills, caregivers can provide an engaging learning environment that fosters critical thinking. These games range from simple puzzles and riddles to more complex strategy games requiring planning and analysis. Each game presents a unique opportunity for children to exercise their cognitive abilities.

Problem-solving skills are essential for navigating the challenges of everyday life, and by introducing children to different types of cognitive games, caregivers can help them develop these crucial skills early on. Games that require logical reasoning, pattern recognition, and creative thinking can enhance problem-solving capabilities. It's essential to offer a variety of games to keep children interested and engaged while also providing opportunities for them to tackle different types of problems.

Through cognitive games, children learn to approach problems systematically, break them into manageable parts, and apply logical reasoning to find solutions. These games stimulate their minds and teach valuable skills they can use in various situations. By integrating these games into teaching strategies, caregivers can create a fun and interactive way for children to develop their problem-solving abilities.

Caregivers should tailor the selection of cognitive games to suit the age and developmental stage of the child. Younger children may benefit from simple matching games or shape puzzles that help build foundational skills. In comparison, older children can engage with more complex challenges that require higher levels of critical thinking. Adapting the difficulty level of the games ensures that children are appropriately challenged while still feeling motivated to participate.

Consistent exposure to cognitive games can have long-lasting benefits for children's problem-solving capabilities. By making these games a regular part of their learning routine, caregivers can help children hone their critical thinking skills over time. Encouraging children to practice these skills through play makes learning enjoyable and instills the confidence to tackle new challenges with resilience and creativity.

In summary, integrating cognitive games into teaching strategies effectively enhances problem-solving capabilities in young children. By offering a diverse range of games that stimulate different aspects of critical thinking, caregivers can support children in developing essential skills for navigating the complexities of the world around them. Through consistent practice and engagement with these games, children can cultivate a strong foundation in problem-solving that will serve them well into the future.

Creating a balanced routine incorporating brain-stimulating activities is essential for nurturing comprehensive cognitive development in young children. Variety is necessary to engage a child's mind and foster critical thinking skills. Introducing a mix of activities that challenge different cognitive functions can help children develop a well-rounded set of skills that will serve them well in various aspects of life.

Incorporating puzzles and brain games into daily activities can be a fun and effective way to stimulate critical thinking. These activities encourage children to think creatively, problem-solve, and think outside the box. By presenting challenges that require logical reasoning and deduction, puzzles and brain games can help children develop their analytical skills while having fun.

Physical activity is also crucial for cognitive development. Encouraging children to engage in activities that require coordination, balance, and spatial awareness can help enhance their mental abilities. Activities such as dancing, sports, or even simple games like hopscotch can improve a child's focus, memory, and problem-solving skills.

Reading is another powerful tool for stimulating young minds. Reading aloud helps children develop language skills and exposes them to new ideas and concepts. Encouraging children to ask questions about the story or predict what might happen next can help foster their critical thinking abilities.

Artistic activities, such as drawing, painting, or crafting, are excellent ways to promote creativity and critical thinking in children. These activities encourage children to express themselves creatively while also honing their problem-solving skills as they figure out how to bring their ideas to life.

Encouraging exploration of the world around them is vital for a child's cognitive development. Taking nature walks, visiting museums, or simply exploring different environments can help children make connections between what they learn in books or at school and the real world.

Setting aside dedicated time for brain-stimulating activities daily ensures children have consistent opportunities to exercise their minds. By making brain-stimulating activities a regular part of their routine, caregivers can help instill a love for learning and critical thinking in young minds.

The Importance of Innovative Teaching Methods

The journey through understanding the significant impact of brain games and puzzles on young minds has underscored a crucial truth: innovative teaching methods are indispensable. These methods do not just supplement traditional education; they are at the core of fostering an environment where critical thinking thrives. Integrating varied cognitive games into daily routines equips children with the problem-solving skills necessary for success in a rapidly evolving world.

Actionable Strategies for Enhanced Cognitive Development

Empowering young learners involves more than just introducing them to new challenges; creating a balanced routine consistently stimulates their cognitive abilities. This balance is not about overwhelming children with endless tasks but about weaving brain-stimulating activities into their day with intention and care. Practical strategies such as puzzle-solving sessions or structured playtime can be seamlessly integrated into educational settings or home environments, ensuring that cognitive development is both comprehensive and engaging.

Encouragement to Take Initiative

Every caregiver and educator has the power to transform learning into a dynamic, interactive process that captivates young minds. You are not alone in this endeavor. Armed with these tools and knowledge, the community of educators and parents can make a profound difference. Take the initiative. Experiment with different games and observe which resonates most with your children or students. Adjust frequencies, difficulty levels, and participation in these activities to suit individual learning curves and watch as critical thinking blossoms.

Foster Curiosity and Exploration

Remember, the goal is to spark curiosity and encourage exploration. Each child's journey will be unique, but the destination remains the same: a well-rounded individual equipped with strong problem-solving capabilities and an agile mind. We prepare our children for school and life by nurturing these skills early on.

Let us embrace these innovative teaching methods with enthusiasm and confidence, knowing they are vital to unlocking immense potential in every young learner. Through commitment and creativity in our approaches, we can ensure that our children grow into curious, capable, and critical thinkers ready to face the future's challenges.

Chapter 13: Crafting Inquisitive Thinkers: The Role of the Guiding Adult

"People who think they know everything are a great annoyance to those of us who do."

Isaac Asimov

Unlocking the Potential of Young Minds Through Strategic Play

Developing critical thinking skills in early childhood is crucial for fostering a generation that is analytical, innovative, and capable of solving complex problems. The significance of guiding young learners through brain-stimulating activities cannot be overstated. As adults—whether educators, parents, or caregivers—we can shape these young minds by integrating brain games and puzzles into their daily routines. These tools are not just playthings but essential instruments in developing cognitive abilities that will serve children throughout their lives.

Brain games and puzzles do more than entertain; they serve as gateways to enhanced cognitive development. By presenting challenges that require thinking and problem-solving, these activities push children to step outside their comfort zones and use their reasoning skills in new ways. This stimulation is vital for brain growth and helps children learn how to approach problems from various angles, fostering flexibility in thinking and enhancing their ability to generate multiple solutions.

A supportive environment is critical to nurturing these skills. Children thrive in spaces that encourage exploration and question-asking without fear of judgment. This chapter emphasizes creating environments where children feel safe expressing their thoughts and curiosity. Adults must be facilitators of learning rather than just providers of knowledge, guiding children through discovery with patience and enthusiasm.

Strategies for adults to effectively guide this learning process are also crucial. It involves knowing when to step in and when to step back, allowing children the space to explore ideas independently. This balance helps foster a sense of independence in young learners, preparing them for academic challenges and real-world problems. It is about distinguishing between providing guidance and allowing enough freedom for self-exploration.

Moreover, fostering curiosity should be a continuous effort. Curiosity drives the desire to learn more deeply and thoroughly. Encouraging questions, experimenting alongside them, and even admitting when we don't know the answers are practices that stimulate an investigative mindset. This approach enriches the learning experience and solidifies the bonds between children and their guiding adults, creating a mutual trust that facilitates deeper learning.

Lastly, practical methods such as incorporating thematic brain games tailored to current lessons or interests can significantly boost engagement and effectiveness. Whether solving math puzzles, arranging story sequences, or navigating mazes that require critical thinking, each activity should serve a clear purpose in developing specific cognitive skills.

By understanding and implementing these strategies, adults can ensure they are equipping young minds with the tools necessary for success in an increasingly complex world. The journey towards becoming reflective thinkers starts with how we nurture our children's intellectual curiosities today. Engaging them with meaningful challenges and mindfully supporting their growth creates a foundation for academic success, lifelong resilience, and adaptability.

Adults play a crucial role in shaping children's cognitive development by guiding them towards becoming analytical and reflective thinkers. Encouraging curiosity and fostering a love for learning are vital strategies to instill inquisitiveness in young minds. Adults can nurture their natural inclination towards discovery and critical thinking by providing children with opportunities to explore, question, and investigate.

Modeling critical thinking is another powerful tool for adults to guide children in developing their analytical skills. Adults can show children the value of thinking deeply about different situations by demonstrating how to approach problems methodically, consider various perspectives, and evaluate information critically. Engaging children in discussions that prompt them to think critically and express their thoughts also helps them refine their reasoning abilities.

Creating an environment that supports risk-taking and emphasizes the process over the outcome is essential for fostering analytical thinking in children. When children feel safe to experiment, make mistakes, and learn from them without fear of judgment, they are more likely to engage in complex problem-solving tasks with confidence. Encouraging persistence in the face of challenges teaches children resilience and the importance of perseverance in reaching solutions.

Integrating brain games, puzzles, and interactive activities into educational routines can stimulate children's cognitive development and reasoning skills. These activities challenge children to think strategically, problem-solve creatively, and enhance their logical reasoning in a fun and engaging manner. By incorporating such activities into daily learning experiences, adults can allow children to practice critical thinking skills actively.

Cultivating Critical Thinking in a Supportive Learning Environment

Creating a supportive and encouraging learning environment for critical thinking is paramount in shaping young minds for a world of wonders. Children thrive when they feel supported and encouraged in their educational pursuits, especially when developing critical thinking skills. As a guiding adult, your role fosters an atmosphere that nurtures curiosity, resilience, and a passion for learning. Establishing a positive and empowering environment can inspire children to explore, question, and think critically about the world around them.

Encouragement is critical in building confidence and motivation in young learners. Praise their efforts and celebrate their successes, no matter how small. Positive reinforcement can go a long way in instilling a growth mindset and encouraging children to tackle challenges enthusiastically. Create a safe space where mistakes are viewed as opportunities for learning rather than failures. Encourage children to experiment, take risks, and learn from their experiences.

Modeling critical thinking is another essential aspect of creating a supportive learning environment. Demonstrate how to approach problems analytically, ask thoughtful questions, and seek solutions through reasoning and logic. By showing children how to think critically, you empower them to develop these skills. Engage in discussions that encourage deep thinking, ideas, and perspectives exploration.

Establishing clear expectations is crucial for fostering critical thinking skills. Set goals that challenge children to think creatively, problem-solve effectively, and communicate their ideas. Provide guidance and scaffolding when needed, allowing room for independent thinking and decision-making. Encourage children to ask questions, seek information, and draw connections between different concepts.

Create a rich learning environment with opportunities for exploration, discovery, and intellectual stimulation. Offer diverse resources, such as books, puzzles, games, and hands-on activities that promote critical thinking skills. Encourage children to explore new interests, experiment with different approaches, and engage in open-ended projects that spark curiosity.

In summary, fostering critical thinking in young learners requires creating a nurturing environment where encouragement, modeling, clear expectations, and rich learning opportunities abound. As a guiding adult, your role shapes children's cognitive development. By providing support, inspiration, and guidance along their journey of discovery, you empower them to become analytical thinkers who approach challenges with confidence and creativity.

Young learners are naturally curious and full of wonder, eager to explore the world around them. As guiding adults, it is essential to nurture this curiosity and foster independence in children, preparing them for future analytical challenges. Encouraging exploration through hands-on activities and open-ended questions can stimulate a child's inquisitiveness, prompting them to seek answers and discover new information independently. Children develop the confidence to tackle unfamiliar problems with creativity and resourcefulness by providing self-directed learning and independent thinking opportunities.

Creating a supportive environment that values curiosity and independence is crucial in shaping young minds for critical thinking. Modeling curiosity as an adult can inspire children to ask questions and seek out knowledge independently. Encourage children to explore their interests by providing resources, books, and tools that align with their passions. By allowing children to take the lead in their learning journey, they develop a sense of ownership over their education, fostering a lifelong love for learning.

Embracing failure as a learning opportunity is critical to promoting independence in young learners. Encourage children to see mistakes as stepping stones toward growth and improvement. By reframing failure as a natural part of the learning process, children become more resilient and willing to take risks in their pursuit of knowledge. Praise effort over outcome, emphasizing the importance of perseverance and determination in overcoming obstacles.

Engage children in open-ended discussions that encourage critical thinking and problem-solving skills. Pose thought-provoking questions that challenge children to think beyond surface-level answers. Encourage divergent thinking, where multiple solutions are welcomed, fostering creativity and innovation in young minds. By promoting a culture of inquiry and exploration, children can analyze complex problems from various perspectives.

Provide opportunities for hands-on experimentation that allow children to test hypotheses and draw conclusions based on evidence. Activities such as science experiments, building projects, or art creations enable children to apply critical thinking skills in real-world scenarios. Encourage reflection on their experiences, prompting children to think critically about their processes and outcomes.

In preparing young learners for future analytical challenges, it is essential to instill a sense of curiosity, independence, and resilience early on. By nurturing these qualities through hands-on activities, open-ended discussions, and a supportive learning environment, guiding adults plays a vital role in shaping the next generation of analytical thinkers. Encouraging children to explore, question, experiment, and reflect empowers them to approach challenges confidently and creatively, laying a solid foundation for lifelong learning and critical thinking skills.

Guiding young minds towards critical thinking is not just beneficial—it's essential. By fostering an environment where children are encouraged to analyze and reflect, adults play a pivotal role in nurturing future generations capable of facing complex challenges with innovative solutions. The strategies discussed offer practical ways to incorporate analytical and reflective thinking into everyday interactions with children.

Supportive environments are fundamental in encouraging young learners to embrace and not fear critical thinking challenges. Creating spaces where children feel safe to question, explore, and make mistakes is vital. This nurturing approach leads to greater independence and confidence in their cognitive abilities.

Fostering curiosity should be at the heart of our efforts. Children are naturally driven to learn and understand more about their world when they are curious. This intrinsic motivation prepares them for the analytical tasks they will face later. Encouraging independence through guided activities allows children to explore their thoughts and ideas in a structured yet open-ended way.

The role of brain games and puzzles cannot be overstated—they are potent tools that sharpen reasoning skills while making the process engaging and fun. These activities challenge young minds, teaching them to think strategically and solve problems effectively. Regularly including such games in educational routines enhances cognitive development and makes learning a joyful experience.

Every interaction with a child can impact their future critical thinking abilities. Adults can significantly influence how children perceive and interact with the world around them by taking deliberate steps to integrate thoughtful questioning, supportive feedback, and engaging brain exercises.

Let's embrace these strategies confidently, knowing each small step contributes to the more significant journey of preparing adept, reflective thinkers for tomorrow's challenges.

Chapter 14: Tomorrow's Thinkers: Nurturing Resilient and Adaptable Minds

"It's not what you look at that matters, it's what you see."

Henry David Thoreau

Empowering Tomorrow's Leaders: The Indispensable Role of Early Critical Thinking

At the core of modern education lies an undeniable truth: early childhood is a critical period for developing thinking skills that resonate throughout a person's academic and professional life. Educators and caregivers have the remarkable opportunity to guide young learners not just to think but to think critically and analytically about the world around them. This nurturing of inquisitive minds forms the backbone of their future resilience and adaptability.

Critical thinking in early childhood sets the stage for lifelong learning and problem-solving capabilities. It enables children to process information deeply, analyze scenarios, and make informed decisions. Such skills are beneficial and essential in a world where change is the only constant. As we delve deeper into the implications of fostering these abilities, it becomes clear that the benefits extend beyond academic success, touching every aspect of personal and professional life.

In preparing children for future challenges, it's crucial to understand the evolving landscape of the job market. Skills forecasted as necessary for tomorrow include problem-solving, emotional intelligence, adaptability, and technological literacy—competencies rooted deeply in critical thinking. By embedding these skills early on, caregivers ensure that children are ready and eager to navigate complex environments.

Moreover, a mindset geared towards continuous improvement is indispensable in today's fast-paced world. Instilling this mindset from a young age fosters a lifelong passion for learning and self-development. It encourages children to see challenges as growth opportunities and approach problems with creativity and resilience.

The strategies discussed throughout this book aim to integrate critical thinking into daily interactions with preschool-aged children without overwhelming them or underestimating their potential. Simple practices like asking open-ended questions, encouraging exploration, and discussing various outcomes significantly develop young analytical minds.

As we approach the end of our journey through Critical Beginnings, it becomes evident how intertwined these themes are with the overarching goal of empowering young minds. By understanding and implementing the tactics shared, caregivers can confidently create environments that promote curiosity, analysis, and an eagerness to learn.

Each chapter has built upon the last, culminating in a comprehensive toolkit that supports the development of essential cognitive skills from a tender age. The insights provided here are theoretical and practical steps that any caregiver can take to impact their child's future capabilities profoundly.

Thus, by fostering an environment rich in opportunities for critical engagement, we actively prepare our youngest generation to face and shape the future. Their journey through learning and adaptation begins with our commitment to their early cognitive development—a commitment that promises to yield dividends in their lifelong pursuit of knowledge and innovation.

Early critical thinking skills are not just academic tools but essential for success. When children are encouraged to think critically from a young age, they develop the ability to analyze situations, solve problems, and make informed decisions. These skills go beyond the classroom, shaping how individuals approach challenges and opportunities. By fostering critical thinking early on, caregivers and educators lay the foundation for a lifetime of learning and growth.

Research has shown that children exposed to critical thinking exercises at an early age demonstrate improved academic performance. Children strengthen their cognitive abilities and problem-solving skills by engaging in activities requiring them to think independently. These benefits extend beyond the educational realm, influencing how children approach real-world situations and navigate complex challenges.

Critical thinking is not about memorizing facts but about understanding concepts deeply. When children learn to question information, evaluate evidence, and draw logical conclusions, they become better equipped to face uncertainties and make sound judgments. These skills are invaluable in an ever-changing world where adaptability and resilience are vital for success.

Encouraging children to think critically also nurtures their creativity and curiosity. When young minds are encouraged to explore ideas freely and think outside the box, they develop a sense of wonder and a thirst for knowledge that propels them toward continuous learning. This natural curiosity drives growth and development, instilling a lifelong love for exploration and discovery.

The benefits of early critical thinking skills extend beyond individual success; they contribute to building a society of resilient thinkers who can tackle complex issues collaboratively. By nurturing critical thinking in children, caregivers and educators empower them to become active participants in shaping a better future for themselves and others. The ripple effect of fostering critical thinking early on can lead to positive changes in communities and societies.

Nurturing Critical Thinking for Future Success

The demand for adaptable and critical thinkers is rising in today's rapidly evolving job market. As technology continues to reshape industries and professions, the ability to navigate uncertainty and solve complex problems becomes increasingly valuable. Critical thinking is a cornerstone for future readiness, enabling individuals to analyze information, think creatively, and make informed decisions in dynamic environments.

Future job roles are projected to require skills beyond technical expertise, emphasizing the need for individuals who can adapt to changing circumstances and innovate effectively. Employers seek candidates who can approach challenges with a critical eye, evaluate multiple perspectives, and propose innovative solutions. Critical thinking becomes a distinguishing factor in a competitive job market, setting apart those who can thrive in ambiguity from those who struggle to adapt.

Integrating critical thinking in education equips individuals with the tools to succeed in diverse career paths. By fostering a mindset of curiosity and exploration from an early age, caregivers and educators lay the foundation for children to become agile thinkers capable of navigating complex problems. Encouraging children to question assumptions, seek alternative solutions, and engage in reflective analysis prepares them for the uncertainties of tomorrow's professional landscape.

Adaptable minds are more likely to embrace change and view challenges as opportunities for growth. Cultivating critical thinking skills enables individuals to approach obstacles with resilience and determination rather than succumbing to defeat. By instilling a sense of intellectual curiosity and a willingness to learn from failures, caregivers empower children to develop a growth mindset that propels them toward success in an ever-changing world.

As industries continue to evolve rapidly, thinking critically will be indispensable. Individuals who can adapt quickly, problem-solve effectively, and clearly communicate complex ideas will be at the forefront of innovation. Nurturing these skills in children from an early age ensures they are well-prepared to meet the challenges of an uncertain future with confidence and competence.

Incorporating critical thinking into educational practices is not just about preparing children for specific jobs but equipping them with essential life skills. The capacity to analyze information critically, make sound judgments, and communicate effectively transcends professional boundaries, impacting every aspect of an individual's life. By emphasizing these skills in educational settings, caregivers set children on a path toward lifelong learning and personal development.

The future belongs to those who can adapt, innovate, and think critically. By nurturing resilient and adaptable minds through early exposure to critical thinking skills, caregivers play a pivotal role in shaping the next generation of thinkers and innovators. Encouraging children to explore their curiosity, question assumptions, and engage with complexity prepares them for future careers and a life filled with possibilities and opportunities.

As we prepare children for an uncertain future, cultivating a mindset of continuous improvement and learning is paramount. Encouraging resilience and adaptability in young minds equips them with the tools needed to navigate challenges and opportunities that lie ahead. In fostering this mindset, caregivers and educators can instill a sense of curiosity and a hunger for knowledge that will serve children well throughout their lives.

Embracing a Growth Mindset: One key aspect of nurturing a culture of continuous improvement is promoting a growth mindset. Teaching children that abilities can be developed through dedication and hard work helps them approach challenges with optimism and perseverance. By praising effort rather than inherent talent, caregivers can empower children to see setbacks as opportunities for growth and learning.

Fostering Curiosity: Curiosity is the fuel that drives continuous learning. Encouraging children to ask questions, explore new ideas, and seek out answers sparks their innate sense of wonder and propels them toward more profound understanding. Creating an environment where curiosity is celebrated cultivates a love for learning that transcends formal education.

Embracing Failure as a Learning Opportunity: In a world where success is often equated with perfection, reframing failure as a natural part of the learning process is crucial. Teaching children to embrace failure as an opportunity for growth helps them develop resilience and problem-solving skills. By normalizing setbacks and encouraging perseverance, caregivers can empower children to bounce back stronger after encountering obstacles.

Promoting Lifelong Learning: Continuous improvement extends beyond the classroom walls. Encouraging children to see learning as a lifelong pursuit fosters adaptability in the face of change. Modeling a commitment to ongoing education and personal growth sets a powerful example for children, showing them that curiosity knows no bounds and that there is always more to discover.

Encouraging Self-Reflection: Helping children develop the habit of self-reflection nurtures metacognitive skills essential for continuous improvement. Encouraging them to assess their strengths and weaknesses, set goals, and track their progress instills a sense of agency over their learning journey. By fostering self-awareness, caregivers empower children to take ownership of their development.

Creating Supportive Networks: Surrounding children with supportive networks of peers, mentors, and role models reinforces the value of continuous improvement. Building communities that champion growth, celebrate achievements, and provide guidance during challenges creates a safety net for children navigating the complexities of learning and personal development.

In cultivating a mindset of continuous improvement and learning in children, caregivers lay the foundation for resilient, adaptable thinkers ready to tackle whatever the future may hold. By fostering curiosity, embracing failure as an opportunity for growth, promoting lifelong learning, encouraging self-reflection, and creating supportive networks, caregivers equip young minds with the tools needed to thrive in an ever-changing world.

As we reach the close of our exploration into the profound impact of nurturing critical thinking from the earliest stages of childhood, it is clear that educators and caregivers hold the keys to unlocking a world of potential in young minds. By fostering an environment where inquiry and analysis are encouraged and celebrated, we empower children to become resilient and adaptable thinkers—indispensable qualities in navigating the complexities of tomorrow's world.

The long-term benefits of early critical thinking are undeniable. Children equipped to assess situations critically, solve problems creatively, and adapt to changing scenarios stand a better chance at academic success and personal fulfillment. These skills lay a robust foundation for lifelong learning, ensuring our young learners are prepared for predictable challenges and unforeseen opportunities.

Looking ahead, the job market continues to evolve rapidly, influenced by technological advancements and global interconnectedness. The skills forecasted to be most valuable—problem-solving, adaptability, and analytical thinking—are precisely those developed through early critical thinking initiatives. By prioritizing these skills today, we are effectively future-proofing our children's careers and contributing to an innovative, dynamic, and resilient workforce.

Furthermore, cultivating a continuous improvement mindset is perhaps our most crucial task. In an unpredictable world, the ability to learn from experiences and persistently enhance one's own skills is invaluable. Instilling this mindset in children from a young age fosters a love for learning that transcends the classroom and permeates every aspect of life.

Throughout this book, we have equipped you with practical strategies to integrate critical thinking into daily interactions with preschool-aged children without overwhelming them or underestimating their capabilities. These strategies are designed to enhance cognitive development, build confidence, and spark curiosity—traits that fuel further exploration and discovery.

By understanding your pivotal role in shaping these young minds, you can approach this responsibility with reverence and enthusiasm. It is a journey filled with wonder, challenge, and profound growth—not just for the children you guide but for yourself.

So, let us move forward with purpose and passion, knowing that each small step we take in fostering critical thinking in early childhood is a giant leap towards preparing a generation for success in whatever future they choose to create. Let's commit to being proactive architects of supportive learning environments where every child can thrive as a thinker, learner, and innovator. Together, we can look forward to a world enriched by their contributions—a world reimagined through their eyes.

Epilogue

"I cannot teach anybody anything, I can

only make them think."

Socrates

The Journey Forward: Empowering Young Minds

As we conclude this exploration into the development of critical thinking in young children, it's essential to reflect on how this knowledge can be seamlessly integrated into daily life. Whether you are a parent, educator, or caregiver, the strategies outlined in this book offer practical ways to nurture a child's curiosity and analytical skills from an early age.

Critical thinking is more than an academic skill; it is a lifelong tool that empowers individuals to analyze, question, and understand the world around them. By fostering these skills early, we lay a robust foundation for children to handle complex problems and make thoughtful decisions.

Throughout this book, we've discussed various methods and activities designed to engage preschool-aged children in critical thinking. From simple questioning techniques to structured problem-solving exercises, these strategies are tailored to be engaging and effective for young learners.

To ensure these concepts are understood and applied, consider setting regular times each week to practice these activities. Integration into everyday routines—like during playtime or while reading stories—can make learning natural and enjoyable for children. Remember, consistency is critical in building strong cognitive abilities.

While this guide provides a comprehensive framework for nurturing critical thinking, it is not exhaustive. The field of early childhood education continually evolves, and so should our approaches. I encourage you to keep exploring, experimenting with new ideas, and staying informed about the latest research in cognitive development.

Now is the time to take action. Armed with knowledge and strategies from this book, you have the power to make a significant impact on the developmental journey of the children in your care. Each small step you take can lead to great strides in their growth and understanding.

Let us leave with a lasting thought that underscores the importance of our mission:

"Education is not the filling of a pail,

but the lighting of a fire."

William Butler Yeats

This quote beautifully captures what we aim to achieve—igniting a spark of curiosity and critical thinking in young minds that will illuminate their paths for years. Let's commit ourselves to this noble task enthusiastically and hope for a brighter future shaped by thoughtful, curious minds.

Conclusion

"A great many people think they are thinking when they are merely rearranging their prejudices."

William James

In the concluding remarks of our exploration into nurturing critical thinking in the early years, it's paramount to revisit the essence of our mission. We embarked on this journey with a vision to equip young minds with the tools for academic success and navigating the complexities of the real world. The strategies and insights shared within these pages are stepping stones towards a future where critical thinking and creativity are integral to our children's lives.

Reflecting on the contents, it's clear that fostering a love for learning and critical thinking is not a solitary endeavor. It requires a collaborative effort among parents, educators, and caregivers. Each plays a pivotal role in shaping the environment in which our children grow and learn. Through our shared dedication, we can create a nurturing space that encourages curiosity, problem-solving, and the joy of discovery.

The detailed practical strategies and activities serve as a foundation for building. They are not prescriptive but rather suggestive, inviting continuous experimentation and adaptation. The dynamic nature of education, much like the world around us, demands that we stay curious, open-minded, and committed to learning alongside our children.

As we look toward the future, the significance of critical thinking becomes even more pronounced. In a rapidly changing world, the ability to adapt, analyze, and approach challenges creatively will be paramount to personal and professional success. We are setting our children on lifelong learning and resilience by instilling these skills from a young age.

However, the pursuit of fostering critical thinking is not without its challenges. It requires patience, persistence, and a deep understanding of each child's individual needs. There is no one-size-fits-all solution but rather a tapestry of experiences that contribute to the growth and development of young learners. Our role is to guide, support, and encourage, always mindful of the unique light within each child that awaits kindling.

In closing, the call to action for each of us involved in the developmental journeys of children is to approach this task with hope, dedication, and a sense of wonder. The impact of our efforts may not always be immediately visible, but every small step taken is a leap toward a brighter, more thoughtful world.

- Foster a collaborative environment among parents, educators, and caregivers to support children's development.
- Use the strategies and activities as a foundation, but remain flexible and adaptable.
- Stay committed to the continuous exploration and application of new ideas in education.
- Remember the importance of patience and understanding in nurturing individual growth.
- Keep the ultimate goal in sight: equip children for academic success and a fulfilling, resilient life.

In conclusion, we move forward knowing that our efforts today light the path for tomorrow's thinkers, innovators, and leaders. It is a profound responsibility and privilege to ignite the spark of curiosity and critical thinking in young minds, shaping a future where they not only thrive but excel in the face of challenges yet unseen.

Bonus Material

Your Questions, Answered!

1. How Do You Differentiate Between Teaching Critical Thinking Skills and Traditional Teaching Methods?

Teaching critical thinking skills diverges significantly from traditional teaching methods, primarily through its focus on fostering independent thought, analytical reasoning, and the ability to question and evaluate information critically. Conventional teaching methods often emphasize rote memorization and the passive reception of information, where students are expected to absorb knowledge presented by the teacher without questioning its validity or exploring its application in various contexts. This approach can limit students' ability to think independently and adaptively apply their knowledge to solve real-world problems.

In contrast, educators encourage students to engage actively with the material when teaching critical thinking skills. This involves presenting scenarios or problems requiring students to apply logical reasoning, analyze evidence, distinguish between facts and opinions, and synthesize information from various sources to form conclusions. Such an approach is dynamic and student-centered, placing the learners at the heart of the educational process. It promotes a deeper understanding of the subject matter, as students are not merely memorizing facts but learning how to apply them in various situations, understand their implications, and assess their value.

Furthermore, teaching critical thinking facilitates the development of essential life skills, including problem-solving, decision-making, and the ability to engage in reflective thought. It prepares students for the complexities of the natural world, where answers are not always clear-cut or readily available. This methodology considers mistakes valuable learning opportunities rather than failures, encouraging resilience and perseverance. This approach requires a more flexible classroom environment, where open dialogue, questions, and debates are encouraged, and educators serve more as guides than as sources of undisputed knowledge.

In summary, teaching critical thinking skills represents a paradigm shift from traditional teaching methods. It focuses on developing robust cognitive tools that enable students to approach the information critically and creatively. Doing so enhances their academic success and equips them with the competencies necessary for lifelong learning and success in their personal and professional lives. This methodology acknowledges the evolving needs of the modern world. It seeks to prepare students to absorb knowledge and continuously engage with and contribute to the world around them.

2. Can Critical Thinking Skills Be Taught to Children of Any Age, or Is There an Ideal Age to Start?

The concept that critical thinking skills can be imparted to children of any age is founded on recognizing that these abilities are inherent and developed. Children exhibit natural curiosity and question the world around them from an early age, making it an ideal time to start nurturing these inclinations into structured critical thinking skills. It isn't about waiting for a specific age when a child is deemed 'ready' for complex thinking processes; instead, it's about adapting the complexity and manner of critical thinking exercises to match their developmental stage. From simple problem-solving activities in preschoolers to more sophisticated analytical discussions with older children, every age offers a unique opportunity for cultivating these skills.

Starting early capitalizes on the young brain's plasticity, which is exceptionally receptive to new learning experiences. This early introduction to critical thinking does not mean imposing overly complex problems onto young children but integrating age-appropriate essential thinking activities into their daily learning. For younger children, this might involve asking open-ended questions that encourage them to think about 'why' and 'how' things happen or providing scenarios that require them to make choices and then discuss the reasons behind their decisions. This foundational work lays the groundwork for more advanced critical thinking as they grow older, with their challenges evolving in complexity to include formal logic, hypothesis testing, and the evaluation of arguments, among others.

Furthermore, developmental psychology and education research suggest that critical thinking skills are not tied to a specific age but can be developed and enhanced at any point in life. What changes with age is the approach and the depth of critical thinking. Encouraging critical thinking from a young age promotes academic success and instills a mindset that is inquisitive, reflective, and capable of independent problem-solving. This approach ensures that by the time children reach adulthood, they possess a well-honed toolkit of critical thinking skills, prepared to tackle the challenges of the real world. This holistic view of education underscores the indispensable role of teachers and parents in recognizing and nurturing each child's potential from a very early age, facilitating a transition from natural curiosity to structured, reflective, and productive thinking habits.

3. What Are the Most Common Barriers Parents and Educators Face When Trying to Instill Critical Thinking in Children?

One of the primary barriers parents and educators encounter when fostering critical thinking in children is the traditional education model, which often emphasizes rote memorization over analytical thinking. In many educational settings, there is a strong focus on acquiring and recalling information rather than understanding underlying concepts and applying knowledge in various contexts. This approach can inadvertently discourage questioning and independent thought, key components of critical thinking. Students may become accustomed to seeking the "right" answers to pass tests rather than developing the skills to analyze problems critically and formulate solutions.

Another significant challenge is the lack of resources and support for implementing critical thinking exercises into the curriculum. Educators, who are often pressured to cover a vast syllabus within a limited time, may find it challenging to allocate time for activities promoting critical thinking. Integrating these skills into everyday learning becomes daunting without adequate training and resources. This situation is compounded by standardized testing systems prioritizing content recall over creative and analytical thought, leaving little room for educators to deviate from prescribed teaching methods.

Furthermore, in today's fast-paced digital age, children are bombarded with information from various sources, including social media, which can overwhelm their ability to critically assess what they see and hear. This information overload can hinder their ability to concentrate, evaluate, and reflect deeply on the content. Parents and educators face the additional task of teaching children to navigate this digital landscape effectively, discerning between credible information and misinformation, which is crucial for developing refined critical thinking skills.

In overcoming these barriers, a concerted effort from educators, parents, and policymakers is required to prioritize and integrate critical thinking into the educational framework from an early age. This involves rethinking assessment methods to value process over product, creativity over memorization, and encouraging a classroom environment where questions are welcomed and mistakes are seen as learning opportunities. By addressing these challenges head-on, we can better equip our children with the critical thinking skills they need to succeed in an increasingly complex world.

4. How Can Technology Be Used Effectively to Enhance Critical Thinking Skills in Early Childhood?

When leveraged thoughtfully, technology can significantly bolster the development of critical thinking skills in early childhood. Interactive and digital tools offer unique opportunities for children to engage with concepts actively and apply their knowledge in practical contexts, a foundational aspect of critical thinking. For instance, educational apps and games designed with problem-solving missions encourage children to think critically to overcome obstacles. These digital platforms can adjust complexity to match a child's developmental stage, providing a personalized learning experience that challenges them at the right level.

In addition to interactive games, the internet offers many resources for critical thinking activities. From virtual field trips that introduce children to new cultures and environments to online puzzles that require logical reasoning, the digital world is replete with tools that stimulate a child's curiosity and analytical thinking. Furthermore, technology facilitates collaborative learning, where children can work on projects with peers from around the globe, promoting the development of critical thinking through diverse perspectives and problem-solving techniques. This collaborative effort enhances vital thinking and teaches children the value of teamwork and communication in solving complex issues.

However, effective technology integration into critical thinking exercises requires careful planning and guidance from educators and parents. It is essential to select age-appropriate digital tools that align with learning objectives, ensuring that technology acts as a supplement to, rather than a replacement for, traditional learning methods. Additionally, fostering an environment where children are encouraged to question what they see online and assess the credibility of their sources can further enhance their critical thinking skills. By approaching technology as a tool for active learning and inquiry, educators and parents can support the development of critical thinking skills that are crucial for success in the 21st century.

5. Are There Specific Activities or Games That Can Help Develop Critical Thinking Skills in Young Children?

Indeed, several activities and games are designed to nurture critical thinking skills in young children, promoting their capacity for analytical thinking, problem-solving, and creative expression. These educational and engaging activities allow children to learn and apply critical thinking in enjoyable and meaningful ways. One excellent example is puzzle-based games, which require children to use logic and strategy to complete challenges. These games help develop spatial awareness, pattern recognition, and strategic planning. Puzzles ranging from simple jigsaw pieces to more complex problem-solving games encourage children to think critically and methodically about how pieces fit together to complete a larger picture or achieve a specific objective.

Another impactful category includes role-playing activities, which allow children to explore different scenarios and perspectives, teaching them empathy and decision-making skills. Through role-playing, children can step into various roles and situations that require them to negotiate, solve problems, and make choices based on the information and resources available to them. This method promotes flexible thinking and allows children to explore the consequences of different actions in a controlled, safe environment. By engaging in role-play, children can assess situations from multiple viewpoints and consider alternate outcomes based on their actions.

Board games, too, serve as an excellent tool for developing critical thinking. Many board games require strategic thinking, foresight, tactical decision-making, and the capacity to anticipate opponents' moves. Games that involve strategy and planning, such as chess, checkers, and even some modern strategic games, teach children to analyze situations, plan ahead, and adjust their approach in response to changing circumstances. These games challenge children to think critically, make decisions based on logic and evidence, and develop resilience by learning from losses and setbacks.

Science experiments and STEM (Science, Technology, Engineering, and Mathematics) projects also play a crucial role in fostering critical thinking. By engaging in hands-on scientific inquiries and projects, children learn to pose questions, form hypotheses, conduct experiments, and draw conclusions based on their observations. This process educates children on the scientific method, encouraging a systematic approach to problem-solving and a deep understanding of cause-and-effect relationships.

In summary, activities and games that stimulate critical thinking provide children an engaging platform to develop essential life skills. These activities, ranging from puzzles and role-playing to board games and scientific inquiries, offer diverse opportunities for children to apply and practice critical thinking in various contexts. By integrating these exercises into educational curricula and home environments, parents and educators can significantly enhance children's analytical, problem-solving, and creative thinking abilities. These skills are invaluable, laying the foundation for lifelong learning and success in an increasingly complex world.

6. What Role Does Emotional Intelligence Play in Developing Critical Thinking Abilities?

Emotional intelligence, often referred to as emotional quotient (EQ), is the ability to recognize, understand, and manage one's own emotions as well as the emotions of others. This concept plays a pivotal role in developing critical thinking abilities, directly influencing how we interpret and interact with the world around us. The link between emotional intelligence and critical thinking is grounded in the understanding that emotions can significantly affect our decision-making processes, problem-solving skills, and communication with others.

By developing high emotional intelligence, individuals learn to manage their emotions, leading to clearer thinking and better problem-solving capabilities. For example, someone who can effectively manage frustration or stress is likelier to tackle complex problems with a calm, clear head, enabling them to think more critically and develop practical solutions. Additionally, emotional intelligence fosters empathy, which is essential to understanding different perspectives and needs. This empathetic understanding is invaluable in critical thinking as it allows for a more comprehensive analysis of situations, including recognizing potential biases and considering various viewpoints.

Furthermore, emotional intelligence enhances communication skills, which is vital for collaborative problem-solving and exchanging ideas. It enables people to express their thoughts and listen actively, fostering an environment where ideas can be shared, debated, and improved. This exchange of diverse perspectives enriches the critical thinking process and cultivates a culture of learning and growth. In group settings, a high EQ can mediate conflicts and find common ground, which is essential for moving forward in complex issues requiring collective reasoning.

Emotional intelligence lays the foundation for critical thinking by providing the emotional stability and understanding necessary to approach problems logically and collaboratively. It equips individuals with the tools to dissect complex issues, understand the emotional underpinnings of different viewpoints, and communicate effectively, ensuring that critical thinking is balanced and inclusive. By integrating EQ-focused practices into education and professional development, society can foster analytically proficient and emotionally intelligent individuals ready to tackle the challenges of the 21st century with empathy and clarity.

7. How Can We Measure the Development of a Child's Critical Thinking Skills Over Time?

Measuring the development of a child's critical thinking skills over time can be approached through various methods, each providing insights into different facets of critical thinking growth. The most effective evaluations often blend qualitative and quantitative measures to comprehensively depict a child's analytical progress.

One approach to gauging critical thinking development is observing and documenting a child's participation in problem-solving activities and discussions. Educators and parents can note instances where the child demonstrates vital critical thinking skills such as questioning assumptions, analyzing information, identifying biases, and considering alternative solutions. For example, during group projects or discussions, a child's ability to listen to others, ask insightful questions and propose reasoned arguments can be indicators of critical thinking maturity. Keeping a record of these observations over time allows for a qualitative assessment of growth in these areas.

Standardized tests designed to measure reasoning abilities and problem-solving skills can provide quantitative data on a child's critical thinking development. These tests assess cognitive skills, including pattern recognition, logical reasoning, and applying principles to new situations. While such tests can offer a snapshot of a child's analytical abilities at a point in time, tracking scores over multiple testing periods can indicate development. However, it's important to contextualize these scores within a broader understanding of the child's learning environment, opportunities for skill application, and individual learning styles.

Incorporating critical thinking assessments into classroom and home learning activities can also be a practical method for evaluating progress. Activities designed to challenge a child's critical thinking, such as strategic games, complex problem-solving tasks, or open-ended discussions on various topics, provide direct opportunities for application and observation. By reviewing a child's approach and solutions to these tasks over time, educators and parents can identify areas needing further development and how a child's critical thinking ability evolves in complexity and depth.

Ultimately, measuring the development of critical thinking skills in children is an ongoing and dynamic process. It requires a balanced combination of observing behaviors, engaging with the child's thought processes, and utilizing formal assessment tools. This multi-faceted approach tracks progress and supports the continuous development of critical thinking abilities by identifying strengths and areas for further growth. Through consistent and thoughtful assessment, educators and parents can provide targeted feedback and strategies to nurture a child's analytical capabilities, preparing them for the complexities of the modern world.

8. In What Ways Can Caregivers Integrate Critical Thinking Exercises Into Everyday Routines?

Caregivers can seamlessly incorporate critical thinking exercises into daily routines by transforming ordinary activities into opportunities for exploration and questioning. This approach nurtures a child's analytical skills and integrates learning naturally into their everyday life, making it both fun and impactful.

Starting with simple conversations, caregivers can encourage children to think critically by asking open-ended questions that prompt them to explain their reasoning, consider different outcomes, or predict the consequences of their actions. For instance, during meal preparation, a caregiver might ask, "What do you think will happen if we don't follow the recipe?" or "Why do you think this ingredient is important?" Such questions stimulate a child's curiosity and encourage them to explore cause-and-effect relationships.

In addition, incorporating problem-solving tasks into playtime is an excellent way to promote critical thinking. Strategic games, puzzles, and building projects challenge children to plan, make decisions, and adjust their strategies based on the outcomes they observe. Caregivers can enhance this experience by engaging in reflective discussions after these activities, asking questions like, "What worked well in your approach?" or "If you could try again, what would you do differently?" This reflection reinforces the learning process and encourages children to think more deeply about their choices and implications.

Another practical method involves role-playing and imaginative play, which allow children to explore various perspectives and develop empathy. By assuming different roles, children learn to understand other viewpoints, an essential critical thinking component. Caregivers can facilitate this by creating scenarios that prompt children to solve a problem as a character, offering insights into different ways of thinking and understanding the world around them.

Caregivers set the stage for continuous learning and development by embedding critical thinking exercises into daily activities. This approach makes building essential thinking skills engaging and relevant. It equips children with the tools to analyze, question, and understand the world more nuanced and comprehensively.

9. What Are Some Examples of Critical Thinking Milestones We Should Expect at Different Developmental Stages?

Critical thinking milestones vary across developmental stages as children's cognitive, emotional, and social skills evolve. In the early years, milestones may include recognizing cause and effect, understanding that actions have consequences, and asking "why" questions to explore the world around them. This curiosity-driven inquiry marks the foundational stage of critical thinking, where the child starts to grasp the basics of reasoning and problem-solving.

Critical thinking skills become more refined as children transition into preschool and early elementary years. During this stage, children can compare and contrast information, categorize objects based on specific attributes, and understand the sequencing of events. They also begin to develop the skills necessary for basic problem-solving and can follow two to three-step directions. Engaging in imaginative play during this stage helps foster these skills as children envision different scenarios and outcomes, a critical component of strategic thinking.

Critical thinking skills take on more complex forms upon reaching middle childhood and adolescence. Children start to think more abstractly and logically, analyzing information more profoundly and considering multiple perspectives before drawing conclusions. They learn to construct more sophisticated arguments, identify logical fallacies, and apply critical thinking skills across domains such as mathematics, science, and reading comprehension. Children can also better appreciate the nuances of moral reasoning at this stage, recognizing that ethical dilemmas often do not have clear-cut answers and that different people may have valid reasons for opposing views.

Throughout these stages, educators and caregivers must provide children with opportunities that match their developmental capabilities while challenging them to stretch their critical thinking skills further. By understanding the expected milestones at each stage, adults can tailor activities and discussions to promote deeper analytical thinking, encourage an understanding of complex concepts, and support the child's overall cognitive growth. This strategic support helps ensure children have the critical thinking abilities to navigate an increasingly complex world with confidence and competence as they grow.

10. How Can Critical Thinking Skills Help Children With Learning Difficulties or Special Education Needs?

Critical thinking skills are particularly beneficial for children with learning difficulties or special education needs, as they provide a framework for understanding complex problems and developing solutions that may not be immediately obvious. These skills enable children to approach challenges systematically, breaking them into manageable parts and considering various solutions. Critical thinking offers alternative pathways to understand and engage with material for children struggling with traditional learning methods. By learning to ask insightful questions and explore different outcomes, children with learning difficulties can gain a deeper understanding of the subjects at hand, potentially bypassing the barriers posed by their challenges.

Furthermore, critical thinking fosters resilience and

adaptability—invaluable qualities for children with special education needs. It encourages them to examine and reflect on their thought processes and to understand that there may be multiple ways to approach a problem. This mindset can help reduce frustration as children learn that initial failure is not an endpoint but part of a process of exploration and discovery. Additionally, the skills involved in critical thinking, such as analyzing arguments, identifying assumptions, and evaluating evidence, can be particularly empowering for these children. They learn to accept information passively and engage actively with content, ask questions, and express their ideas, enhancing their autonomy and confidence in learning settings.

Incorporating critical thinking into the learning experiences of children with special educational needs requires thoughtful adaptation and support from educators and caregivers. Activities designed to build these skills should be aligned with the child's individual capabilities and interests, providing just enough challenge to stimulate engagement without leading to undue frustration. For example, using visual aids, hands-on activities, and technology can help make abstract concepts more concrete and accessible. Furthermore, creating an inclusive learning environment that encourages risk-taking and values diverse ways of thinking can significantly contribute to developing critical thinking skills in these children. By celebrating unique perspectives and fostering a culture of inquiry, educators can help all learners, including those with learning difficulties, develop the critical thinking abilities essential for success in and out of the classroom.

11. Can You Provide Strategies for Teaching Critical Thinking to Highly Gifted Children?

Teaching critical thinking to highly gifted children necessitates an approach beyond traditional education methods. These children often display a higher capacity for understanding complex ideas, abstract reasoning, and problem-solving from a young age. Therefore, strategies for fostering critical thinking in highly gifted students should cater to their advanced intellectual abilities while addressing their emotional and social development needs.

One effective strategy is to introduce open-ended problems that do not have a straightforward solution. This encourages gifted children to explore multiple avenues of thought, consider various perspectives, and engage deeply with the material. For instance, project-based learning can be an excellent way to achieve this, as it allows students to investigate topics of interest comprehensively, applying interdisciplinary approaches. Encouraging these students to take charge of their learning through inquiry-based projects or independent research can significantly enhance their critical thinking abilities.

Another strategy involves promoting metacognitive skills by encouraging students to reflect on their thinking processes. This can be facilitated through discussions, journaling, or any activity requiring students to articulate their thought processes, justify their reasoning, and evaluate the effectiveness of different strategies. Such reflective practices help gifted children become more aware of their cognitive strategy, making them better problem solvers and learners.

Additionally, providing a challenging curriculum significantly different from the standard grade-level content is crucial. This might include advanced literature, complex scientific theories, or higher-level mathematical concepts, coupled with discussions that push them to critically analyze and synthesize information. Embedding ethical dilemmas and moral questions within the curriculum can also enrich gifted students' critical thinking by forcing them to grapple with ambiguity and complexity, encouraging them to develop and defend their viewpoints.

Facilitating opportunities for collaboration among peers with similar intellectual capabilities can further enhance critical thinking skills. Such interactions allow gifted children to be challenged by their peers, exposing them to new ideas and ways of thinking. This social interaction is crucial for talented students to learn how to communicate their ideas effectively, receive constructive feedback, and appreciate the value of diverse perspectives in the problem-solving process. Therefore, creating an educational environment that emphasizes deep, reflective thinking, supported by advanced, interdisciplinary content and peer interaction, is vital to developing the critical thinking abilities of highly gifted children.

12. How Does the Approach to Teaching Critical Thinking Differ Across Cultural Contexts?

Teaching critical thinking across cultural contexts differs significantly due to variations in educational practices, societal values, and communication styles inherent in different cultures. In some cultures, education systems are heavily centered around rote memorization and the reproduction of knowledge, valuing the accumulation of facts over the process of critical analysis and independent thought. In such settings, critical thinking might be introduced as a supplementary skill rather than integrated into the core curriculum, necessitating educators to devise specific strategies that foster these skills within a traditional framework.

Conversely, in cultures where education is viewed through a more constructivist lens, teaching methods are designed to encourage exploration, question-asking, and problem-solving right from the early stages of learning. In these environments, critical thinking is not seen as an additional component but as an essential aspect of learning. Students are engaged in active learning strategies, such as group discussions, problem-based learning, and projects that require analytical thinking and creativity. This approach reflects a cultural value placed on individual autonomy and innovation, fostering a classroom atmosphere where students learn to question, critique, and generate new ideas independently.

Furthermore, the social dimension of learning, which varies greatly between cultures, also influences the teaching methods of critical thinking. For instance, in collectivist societies, group harmony and consensus are highly valued, which can sometimes discourage open debate and individual critique, key components of critical thinking. In such contexts, educators might focus more on collaborative projects that encourage critical reflection within a group setting, allowing for the expression of diverse views in a manner that maintains social harmony. On the other hand, in more individualistic cultures where personal opinion and self-expression are encouraged, teachers may employ strategies that favor debate, individual research projects, and the defense of one's viewpoints, thus directly promoting individual critical analysis and reasoning.

Addressing these cultural nuances is crucial for educators worldwide to effectively teach critical thinking. It requires a thoughtful adaptation of teaching strategies that respect cultural values and learning styles. Educators must be culturally sensitive and innovative, creating a learning environment that fosters critical thinking and aligns with students' cultural contexts. This includes using culturally relevant materials, diversifying teaching approaches, and encouraging students to draw upon their cultural backgrounds and experiences as assets in their critical thinking process. By doing so, teaching critical thinking can become a truly global endeavor, adaptable and relevant across different cultural settings.

13. What Impact Does a Multi-Lingual Environment Have on the Development of Critical Thinking Skills in Children?

A multi-lingual environment significantly impacts the development of critical thinking skills in children, providing a rich, complex backdrop for cognitive development that extends beyond mere language learning. Within such environments, children are exposed to multiple frameworks for understanding the world, which inherently encourages flexibility in thought processes. This linguistic diversity promotes cognitive flexibility, enabling children to easily switch between different modes of thinking and problem-solving strategies. Each language brings cultural nuances, idiomatic expressions, and unique logical structures, challenging children to engage with and reconcile these differences and enhancing their analytical skills.

Furthermore, navigating multiple languages enhances metacognitive abilities; children become acutely aware of their thinking processes as they translate thoughts from one language to another. This constant mental juggling acts as an exercise in critical thinking, as it requires awareness and manipulation of information, evaluation of meaning and context, and applying knowledge in varied linguistic situations. The translation is both linguistic and conceptual, necessitating deep engagement with the material and encouraging children to critically assess and reframe information in different linguistic and cultural contexts.

Bilingual or multilingual individuals often exhibit advanced executive functions, such as problem-solving, planning, and decision-making. Research suggests that the mental discipline required to manage multiple language systems improves these executive functions. It fosters a heightened ability to focus on relevant information and disregard irrelevant distractions, a skill closely linked to practical critical thinking. Dealing with multiple languages daily requires distinguishing subtle differences in meaning, mastering diverse grammatical structures, and understanding cultural contexts that influence language use. These linguistic challenges necessitate analytical thinking and mental flexibility that is beneficial across all realms of learning and cognition.

Additionally, a multi-lingual environment exposes children to diverse perspectives and ways of interpreting the world, which is fundamental to developing empathy and open-mindedness—key components of critical thinking. By understanding and appreciating different cultural contexts and viewpoints through language, children learn to question assumptions, a practice central to critical thinking. This enhances their cognitive skills and prepares them to engage in a globalized world where cross-cultural understanding and communication are invaluable.

In summary, the impact of a multi-lingual environment on the development of a child's critical thinking skills is profound and multifaceted. It goes beyond the acquisition of multiple languages and fundamentally alters cognitive architecture to enhance flexibility, metacognitive awareness, executive functions, and global understanding. Thus, growing up in a multi-lingual environment can be seen as a significant advantage in cultivating critical thinking aptitudes preparing children for complex, multifaceted thinking in their academic pursuits and beyond.

14. Are There Any Recommended Resources or Tools for Parents and Educators to Continue Their Own Education in Teaching Critical Thinking?

For parents and educators aiming to enhance their methods of teaching critical thinking, a wealth of resources and tools is available to support this crucial aspect of a child's education. Books, websites, workshops, and online courses offer a variety of perspectives and strategies designed to integrate critical thinking skills into daily learning activities. One notable resource is the Foundation for Critical Thinking, which provides a wide array of materials, including guides on how to teach children to think critically from a young age. These resources offer practical advice on creating an environment that encourages questioning and open-mindedness, which is crucial for developing critical thinking.

Additionally, incorporating technology into the learning process can be incredibly beneficial. Educational software and apps that enhance logical reasoning, problem-solving, and analytical skills are becoming increasingly popular. These digital tools make learning engaging and accessible, allowing children to practice critical thinking in interactive and fun ways. For example, apps that simulate real-life problem-solving scenarios can help children apply critical thinking skills to everyday challenges, reinforcing these skills outside the classroom.

Workshops and professional development courses for educators also significantly spread effective techniques for teaching critical thinking. These training sessions often cover the latest research in cognitive development and offer strategies for applying this knowledge in the classroom. Participating in these educational opportunities allows teachers to remain current on best practices and innovative methods for fostering an environment conducive to critical thinking.

Furthermore, encouraging a culture of reading and inquiry at home and in educational settings is essential. Engaging with various reading materials, from fiction to non-fiction, exposes children and adults alike to different ideas, perspectives, and problem-solving approaches. Discussion groups, whether in person or online, offer an excellent platform for debating and discussing these ideas, further honing critical thinking skills.

In conclusion, continuing education for parents and educators in teaching critical thinking is vital for equipping children with the skills necessary to succeed in a complex world. By leveraging available resources, incorporating technology, participating in professional development, and fostering a culture of inquiry and discussion, adults can significantly enhance their ability to nurture critical thinking in young minds. These efforts will prepare children for academic success, making informed decisions, and solving real-world problems.

15. How Can Schools and Communities Collaborate to Create an Environment That Fosters Children's Critical Thinking From an Early Age?

Schools and communities play a pivotal role in shaping environments conducive to the growth of critical thinking skills in children. This collaboration is essential, as it extends the cultivation of these skills beyond the classroom and into the broader social environment where children live and play. By working together, they can create a synergistic network of support that encourages children to question, analyze, and think deeply about the world around them from an early age. This partnership involves integrating critical thinking into curricula, extracurricular activities, and community events, providing a consistent message about the importance of these skills across different settings.

One effective strategy for fostering critical thinking is the development of educational programs that encourage inquiry-based learning. Schools can design curricula that challenge students to ask questions, conduct research, and come to their conclusions rather than simply memorize facts. This approach can be supported through community resources such as local libraries, museums, and cultural organizations, offering interactive learning experiences and access to information. For example, community history projects or science fairs that involve research and presentation can motivate children to engage in critical analysis and problem-solving.

Furthermore, professional development for educators is crucial in this partnership. Schools can collaborate with community experts to provide teachers with ongoing training in teaching critical thinking. This might include workshops led by local university faculty or professionals in various fields. Such initiatives help teachers stay abreast of the latest educational strategies and learn from real-world examples of problem-solving and innovation. Educators equipped with these skills can create a classroom environment that supports critical thinking and inspires students to apply these skills in community settings.

Community-wide events and initiatives also offer unique opportunities for promoting critical thinking among young people. Events like public debates, speaker series, and discussion groups can engage children in critical discourse, allowing them to express their views and consider those of others. These experiences help to cultivate a culture of thoughtful analysis and open-mindedness, reinforcing the critical thinking skills learned in the classroom.

In conclusion, the collaboration between schools and communities in fostering an environment that nurtures children's critical thinking from an early age is both vital and multi-dimensional. Integrating critical thinking skills into every aspect of a child's life requires a concerted effort, leveraging educational programs, professional development, and community engagement. By working together, schools and communities can ensure children develop the critical thinking abilities necessary to thrive in an increasingly complex world.

Thank You

We sincerely thank you for dedicating your time to read through this exploration of nurturing critical thinking in our children. Your commitment to understanding and applying these concepts is a decisive step toward cultivating a generation equipped to meet the challenges of our complex world with insight and innovation.

As educators, parents, and community members, we are responsible for fostering environments that encourage questioning, analysis, and thoughtful consideration. May the ideas and strategies presented herein inspire you to implement changes that will enrich the lives of those around you, fostering a culture of critical thinkers ready to contribute positively to society.

Thank you once again for your engagement and dedication to making a difference.

Made in the USA
Las Vegas, NV
09 April 2025